The
Emotionally
Healthy
Leader

Gayle Hardie
& Malcolm Lazenby

MONTEREY
PRESS

First Published in 2013
by Monterey Press
PO Box 319
Carlton North VIC 3054
Australia
www.montereypress.com

Copyright © Gayle Hardie and Malcolm Lazenby, 2013

Author contact: info@globalleadershipfoundation.com
Website: www.globalleadershipfoundation.com

Cover artwork by Trina Stanway
Designed and typeset by Scarab Blue Design

National Library of Australia
Cataloguing-in-Publication entry

Author:	Hardie, Gayle, author.
Title:	The emotionally healthy leader / by Gayle Hardie and Malcolm Lazenby.
ISBN:	9780987581327 (paperback)
Subjects:	Leadership. Mental health. Emotions. Social interaction.
Other Authors/ Contributors:	Lazenby, Malcolm, author.
Dewey Number:	658.4092

To those leaders who want to better understand themselves and their impact on others so they can be more effective as individuals, friends, neighbours and team members, and stewards of communities, organisations, countries and our planet.

Acknowledgements

We value and appreciate the amazing support of a number of people in making this book possible:

The three leaders (Chris, Karenza and Graeme) who provided the context and content for the book and are wonderful examples of emotionally healthy leadership – and yes, they have chosen to use their real names.

John Rogerson, CEO of the Australian Drug Foundation, for the regular and stimulating conversations on leadership and culture, and also for his recurring question: 'So when are you going to put all this in a book?' Just to let you know, John – this is the first instalment.

Russ Hudson and the late Don Riso, pioneers in the world of the Enneagram, for introducing us to levels of development and stimulating our thinking about emotional health in that context.

Dr David Daniels, another Enneagram pioneer, for his untiring interest in who we are and what we are doing to translate the world of emotional health and the Enneagram into business.

Andrea Isaacs, a gifted Enneagram teacher and creator of EnneaMotion, for reinforcing our understanding of emotional health through movement and appreciating that you can't get there simply by thinking.

Sir John Whitmore for challenging our world views as individuals and as leaders.

Dianne and Alan Collins of QuantumThink for being instrumental in our journeys on the emotional health path.

Jack Zenger, former managing director of Zenger Miller, who created six Basic Principles that are integral to the way in which Gayle lives her life.

Greg Goodman, former CEO of RACT, who encouraged and inspired Malcolm to step into his own business around leadership development.

Our Global Leadership Fellows, for leading by example in continuing their own development in emotional health and leadership as well as being on the journey with us.

Trina Stanway for the most creative and thoughtful expression of emotional health on the front cover of the book.

And last, but not least, David Brewster, for literally turning our thoughts and ideas on emotional health into a reality.

Contents

Introduction

Before you start to read this book, we'd like you to pause for a moment and think about leadership. Not the leadership you've read about in management books or the *Harvard Business Review*. Not the *theory* of leadership. We want you to think about real leaders you work with, leaders you have worked for, and leaders you're aware of in the wider community.

We want you to identify two or three of these people who you regard as excellent examples of leaders and leadership. Don't try to analyse them; don't try to pull them apart and work out what makes them stand out. For the moment, bring these people into your imagination. Invite them into a room of your mind and allow them to sit quietly in the corner, serving as constant reminders of what leadership can be when it's done 'right'.

When you've reacquainted yourself with these people – virtually, that is – please read on.

'Leadership' has become a holy grail of the last decade or two. Scores of books, journal articles and research papers have been dedicated to the task of trying to understand what great leadership is and how it might be replicated. There are countless 'shopping lists' of outstanding leadership characteristics, with the implication that all one needs to do to be a better leader is take more of these items off the shelf, that is, to learn more skills.

Yet when we look at leaders in the real world, we see that there is no single 'ideal' of leadership. Leaders, even good and great ones, vary enormously.

Take a look into that room in your mind, at those leaders you've invited inside, and we would be very surprised if you found them to be clones of each other.

Some outstanding leaders are highly charismatic while some are quite reserved. Some bounce into every meeting bursting with energy and ideas, while others are measured and methodical in the way they go about their work. Some are products of wisdom they have acquired over many years; others seem to have been given that wisdom as a childhood birthday gift and apply it to leadership very early in their lives.

Put simply, there is no 'mould' for leadership. Great leaders just 'are' ... or so it sometimes seems.

In this book we want to introduce you to three outstanding leaders we know well. They are, unsurprisingly, all different: they have different personalities, different backgrounds, and work in quite different industries. At the same time, there are powerful aspects of the way they approach leadership that bind them together.

Both individually and collectively, these three leaders represent what we call the 'Emotionally Healthy Leader'.

'What's that?' we hear you ask. 'Is this the new "ultimate" form of leadership – the perfectly balanced set of skills that will make me the leader that everyone looks up to?'

Well, yes. And no.

We do believe that emotionally healthy leadership can have a positive impact – for the leader, on their organisation and in the wider community. In our work, we emphasise the development of emotionally healthy leadership as something that can create a better world.

On the other hand, this is not another 'model' of leadership that, if followed, will make you a great leader. Emotionally healthy leadership does not come from learning new skills. It comes from development of the way you see, respond to and interact with the world. That, we can assure you, is very different from developing a set of skills. In addition, there is a paradox to emotionally healthy leadership in that the more you pursue it for your own benefit, the further away you get from it. Increasing emotional health means increased attention focused on others and less attention on yourself. It is something to aspire to, but not for your own benefit, or to give impetus to your own career progress.

However, we are getting ahead of ourselves. The best way to illustrate emotionally healthy leadership is by example, which is where our three leaders, and our 'portrait', come in.

Later, we will discuss the concept of emotional health in more detail: how high emotional health differs from low emotional health, and what you can do to develop your own emotional health. By the end of this book we hope that you can see a path of leadership development for yourself that will change the way you engage and work with others, strengthening the value of your role as a leader and continuing to bring others along with you on this path.

Part 1:
Portrait of an
Emotionally
Healthy
Leader

A portrait is a likeness – a glimpse inside the soul of the subject. What we hope to give you with the following portrait is a sense of what it is to be an emotionally healthy leader, or to work for or with one. Perhaps you'll be able to imagine working for a leader like this – what the experience would feel like, how effective it would make you in your own work. Perhaps you'll see elements of our portrait in one or more of those leaders seated in your mind right now. Perhaps you'll get a sense of what it might feel like to *be* an emotionally healthy leader.

There is one thing we need to make clear at the outset. One of the characteristics of an emotionally healthy leader is little, if any, distinction between the 'person' and the 'leader'. For that reason you will find that some of the stories and examples we share in the following pages are personal in nature, rather than leadership focused.

Courage

Karenza's grandfather was a big drinker and gambler and had gassed himself in the oven when his son was just 13 years old. That boy, Karenza's father, had grown up on a housing authority estate in Manchester, England, and spent much of his youth moving in and out of various institutions. At around 17 he found himself in front of a magistrate who told him he had two choices: staying on his current path and finding himself in prison before long, or changing course by joining the armed forces. He joined the navy.

When Karenza was about the same age, she also made a choice. Like her dad, she'd been an angry kid. She was kicked out of school more than once and became involved in drug taking. There came a day when she was sitting in a room with a number of other drug takers and was handed a dose of heroin for the first time.

'I remember it vividly. Everyone else stuck it in their arm, and then it was my turn.' She paused. 'I said to myself, "I haven't done this before – am I going to do it or not?" And for probably the first time in my life I realised that I had courage and bravery and could make choices. I didn't have to follow what other people felt was right, or be the norm.'

Karenza got up and left. 'I actually chose to get up and leave and change my life.'

Karenza went back to school – she had to talk her way back in after previously being expelled – and finished her education. She subsequently got a university degree and started building a career, and life, for herself.

Chris was given a very different choice early in his career.

After finishing a business degree, he worked for six years in a sales role. His employer is a small, family-owned, specialist manufacturer with customers around the world.

In 2007 Chris was asked to take on the vacant role of operations manager. This would be an enormous change. It would involve management oversight of the manufacturing group (the factory), engineering, purchasing and so on ... almost every aspect of the business except the part he had been doing to date – sales. To put it mildly, this was going to take Chris outside his comfort zone.

It's fair to say that many people would turn down an opportunity like this. A change to a similar role in a different organisation might be as far as the majority would be prepared to challenge themselves. On the other hand – and Chris himself recognised this – it is also fair to say that most people would not be offered an opportunity like this.

'They said, "You can do this". I was sure they didn't do it without a lot of thought and confidence in me. It was their belief and their support that allowed me to take the job on.'

Since then, Chris has grown into his new role. For someone his age he has a lot of responsibility, including the supervision of a number of people significantly older and more experienced than himself. But Chris has a rare ability to stand back from most challenging situations and take stock before acting – and he has an inner strength that sees him confronting these situations rather than avoiding them.

A small but important example. Recently Chris had to call one of the company's directors to task over a safety issue. Company policy is that safety protection – eye protection, closed shoes, etc. – must be worn by anyone who enters the factory. Any employee who ignores this policy will be disciplined. Yet this director would walk onto the floor wearing open-toed sandals. Chris needed to stop this – it was undermining the factory's safety rules and potentially making them very difficult to enforce.

After a bit of thought, Chris quietly took the director aside and explained the situation. 'I understand that you might think we're becoming a nanny state,' he said, 'but what you are doing undermines everything that I am doing, and what the leaders below me are doing, to enforce professional safety standards and minimise injuries'.

'At the end of the day, you need to be balanced in your processing of everything you hear, but you also have to have a really strong inner belief in what you are doing.'

For over 20 years Graeme has worked in a role many would find simply too difficult. As CEO of a major local council, his role involves constantly navigating the demands of elected councillors (with their often short-term agendas and pet issues), rate payers, his directors and his staff of over 1000.

'Sometimes people say to me, particularly when we are doing something that is unpopular, "I don't know how you can keep smiling, keep your resilience". My view is that you have to have a reasonable level of self-righteousness and inner belief to sustain yourself through this sort of environment.'

Graeme emphasises that the strength he is talking about is not about arrogance or being disconnected.

And in this Graeme picks up a thread that we see as common in the courage demonstrated by all three of our leaders: a courage that is powerfully internal. It's a courage that is reflected in high levels of self-belief but, paradoxically, tempered by enough self-doubt to hold it short of arrogance. It's also a courage that builds on itself with experience. As we shall see in future stories, our three leaders have constantly learnt from their own journeys – successes and failures – and used those lessons to reinforce their inner strength as they have developed.

Balance

The Mallee is a flat, dry region in the north-west of the Australian state of Victoria. This is crop-growing country – largely wheat, canola and barley – though in many respects it has never been ideal for farming. Bordered on the north and west by desert, the area is struck by drought at least once every decade; vicious dust storms can remove swathes of top soil in minutes; floods and bushfires bring their devastation at regular intervals. Even in good years, when the rains are favourable and there is the promise of high yields, a sudden hail storm can decimate wide areas of a carefully nurtured crop in minutes.

This was the country of Graeme's upbringing, on his father's farm. And while it is a region notorious for testing the mettle of the most resilient farmer, Graeme witnessed in his father a willingness to accept the way things were. 'He worried about whether it was going to rain or not, but he would reconcile that by saying, "That's just the way it is". I never got a sense of heightened anxiety in him.'

Whether it is an inherited characteristic or something that Graeme learnt by observation, maintaining a sense of balance and calm regardless of the circumstances is a trait that characterises his leadership. 'Particularly in the life of a CEO, there are a whole lot of things that happen, but at the end of the day there is not a lot of use worrying about things that are outside your control. I'd prefer to put my energies into where I can make a difference.'

That's not to say that Graeme doesn't fear failure. He does, and it is something he is constantly grappling with. What he has developed over the years is the ability to manage and rationalise those fears. 'I have the internal observer constantly questioning, if I am anxious about something, why I am feeling that way.'

Graeme sees the balance he portrays as tempering the reactions of others. 'Those who've worked with me over a period of time recognise that it would be highly unusual for me to overreact, particularly negatively. When the more volatile of my staff know they won't get a volatile reaction from me, my perception is that this has a moderating impact on them.'

At the same time, Graeme is conscious of not coming across as bland or emotionless. 'It's important to be able to take a stand as well.' Graeme takes a hard line on his staff's adherence to their agreed values – he just doesn't see that being firm requires also being over-emotional or hostile.

'Balance' has been a theme in Chris's life for as long as he can remember. He has clear memories of childhood games with his brother, two years younger (Chris is the eldest of four), who was always competitive and liked to play hard. 'I never really needed to get aggressive or fired up because he was always that little bit smaller – I always had the upper hand.'

Recognising and appreciating the value of maintaining perspective and a cool head has helped Chris through a number of taxing stages in his life. His parents split up when he was in his final year of school. 'One of the teachers offered me an extension, "under the circumstances", on an assignment that was due, and I remember wondering what they were talking about. Why would I need an extension?' He later went through a marriage that lasted less than a year. And after turning to distance running as one way of dealing with his separation, he suffered a back injury that has caused him a lot of discomfort and hampered his ability to exercise.

As Chris describes these challenges he doesn't dismiss the emotional impact they have had on him, but at the same time he retains a balanced point of view of them. He doesn't attribute blame; it seems he is more interested in trying to understand and in learning what he can from what has gone before.

Chris believes that his ability to maintain balance and calm was one of the main things his managing director saw in him before offering him the operations management role. In practice this translates as an ability to pause and reflect before coming up with an answer or response. 'I'm not one to fire off without actually thinking about it.'

Nevertheless, for Chris, like Graeme, balance doesn't mean blind acceptance or a lack of responsiveness. Chris is prepared to confront disagreement or conflict rather than let it slide. 'I have had it where two of the directors have had conflicting ideas on something and that's frustrated me. So I have confronted them, asking them to get together and come to a consensus so that we can move forward.'

Karenza has found balance by discovering a willingness to confront herself.

For a long time she 'didn't know what it is like to make myself vulnerable'. Her mantra was 'I am the best' and maintaining that belief meant portraying a powerful, invulnerable presence. This was particularly the case in her role as the relatively new CEO of a non-profit organisation with a mission to 'make a difference in the lives of disenfranchised people'.

However, after a significant relationship break up, Karenza found herself struggling at work. After a few days she could see the looks on the faces of her two general managers. 'I know they were thinking, "What's going on with her?".' So Karenza took what in her eyes was an enormous gamble. She met with her two most senior managers and confided in them.

'I told them what had happened and that I recognised that I was not at the top of my game. I asked them to have my back, and to challenge or question me if they felt I was slipping. It was very hard for me to say this; it felt like I was taking the biggest risk. My fear was that they would look at me and think I was an emotional wreck and an idiot. But I felt that I had to do it.'

Karenza's discovery was that in return for her openness, for her willingness to be vulnerable, a strong bond of trust was built between herself and her managers. 'They stepped up and I grew with that as well. I know it sounds dramatic, but today I would trust both of them with my life.' This opened up a greater sense of balance in Karenza's leadership.

She has also learnt to be more comfortable with being vulnerable. 'I am coming to terms with the reality that I don't need to be the best. I can make a contribution but I don't need to be the best. That's not who I need to be anymore.'

On a day-to-day level, the calm and balance that Graeme and Chris describe do not come easily to Karenza. However, she has discovered a way to find them ... by boxing.

'I box five or six times a week. I always thought boxing was just a dumb sport, but I have never had to think strategy and things so much as when I am in the boxing ring. I am circling my opponent, and thinking about what I am going to do. It's a zone that I've gone into that really is powerful for me. It takes away all the other noise and I just focus in that space.' What Karenza has learnt to do is take a similar approach to a challenge or issue she is grappling with. 'I take it into that space; I see it and circle it and look at it and think what's it going to do and where is it coming in and how am I going to duck and weave around it.'

At the other end of the exercise scale, Karenza also swims regularly, taking a lot out of the rhythmic nature of that activity. 'All the noise and chatter is drowned out, and I give myself time to think.' She has been able to translate the mindset of swimming to her work by occasionally taking herself down to a café when grappling with one issue or other. She orders a coffee and sits quietly on her own for a short while. 'I'm not looking for solutions – which I love to do. I just sit with whatever comes, with my feelings, with what it is.'

While balance may come more readily to Graeme and Chris, exercise plays an important role for them too. Graeme runs or walks four or five times a week; he also emphasises that he maintains good sleep patterns. And while Chris has lately been more restricted to walking, he has swum and run in the past and acknowledges physical exercise as an important contributor to the maintenance of his balance and calm.

Balance, calm, acceptance, trust. While these could be seen as signs of conflict avoidance, our leaders demonstrate that they can be much more than that. Like courage, balance is something that is deeply internal in these leaders. And while it seems to come more easily to some than others, it is not something that is automatic. Chris was aware of the benefits of balance and calm as a child, and is conscious of maintaining that awareness today. Graeme also, while having a naturally calm demeanour, recognises the contribution this makes to his leadership – and the need to constantly nourish it.

Karenza works hard at it because she knows that being irrational and reactive will, more often than not, be counterproductive.

Integrity

Perhaps it is the nature of the complex and ever-changing councillor/ratepayer/executive dynamic that he is managing, but if there is one topic that Graeme feels he needs to return to often, it is the importance of integrity in leadership.

'The most fundamental thing is that leadership is a responsibility; it is not a privilege. If you want to be an authentic, trusted leader you have got to lead by example 24/7. You can't opt for a leadership approach one day that will be different on the next. So that whole level of being consistent – of being transparent in what you stand for, what's important to you and what your expectations are from a leadership point of view – is really, really critical.'

From time to time over the years Graeme has come across what he calls 'cordial hypocrisy': when someone earnestly espouses a set of values or expected behaviours while, in practice, they act in ways quite counter to these.

'That is a real cancer for leadership in my mind. My coaching and mentoring, particularly in my direct reports, is around the notion that no matter what we are doing, who we are doing it with and when we are doing it, we have to be absolutely consistent in reinforcing our leadership style and what we stand for from a leadership point of view. It is not discretionary.'

One of the greatest tests for this is when an elected councillor is seeking assistance from Graeme's team for a particular argument or proposition that person wishes to put to a council meeting. That assistance might be by way of providing background information, statistics and so on that the councillor can use to build their case. 'It is really important that, while being supportive, you also deal with them fairly and equally.' For instance, councillors need to understand that Graeme's team may concurrently be assisting another councillor who is taking up a competing position. 'It's not about taking sides.'

Graeme acknowledges that this can be challenging at times, particularly when he personally believes a particular proposition is fundamentally wrong. He reconciles that by reminding himself that he has done his job by providing advice. '[As elected representatives] it is absolutely their prerogative to make whatever decision they want.'

As a leader, Graeme embraces impartiality and expects it of those working for and with him. Building a culture of integrity was the first task he set himself when he took on his current role over a decade ago.

Karenza has always been driven by her work in youth and community environments. After moving to Australia, this drive and her natural enthusiasm saw her quickly rising through the ranks. 'I found myself in my first CEO gig at 35.' On one level she was feeling great about this. 'My pay packet is increasing, I'm getting status and kudos and all the things that I liked at that time.' On another level – and Karenza freely admits it took a while for her to recognise this – she became caught up in the drama of the role. 'I stopped engaging and thinking proactively; instead I'm just getting frustrated. At that point I have absolutely stopped leading.'

One of Karenza's main challenges was the management of a much older direct report – someone who mistrusted his younger and greener CEO. 'I was unable to win his heart and mind ... and then I couldn't bite the bullet and performance-manage him out.

'I was leading someone I couldn't believe in ... and then I lost faith in the organisation as well.' Ultimately Karenza realised that she was not – and could not – be true to herself inside this organisation so, despite the status she had achieved in the role, she resigned.

The shift to an organisation more consistent with Karenza's values and the personal growth that came with that shift have been central to her ability to achieve. 'I still would have been a CEO [somewhere less aligned with my values]. I still would have done what I have done and I would have got by doing what I knew and did well, but I would not have been successful in the way that I am probably successful now. What I am tasting is a different kind of success; it is a much better success.'

One of the things Chris recognised soon after taking on his operations management role was an us-and-them attitude between different groups in the factory: between the boilermaking team and the fitting team, and between the workshop teams and the office, for instance. This was not something that sat comfortably with Chris, but he recognised that it wasn't something he would be able to remedy overnight. Over time he worked with the various groups, and particularly with their team leaders. Eventually, attitudes started to change. 'I think they themselves recognised that it's not good for them to be in this us-and-them situation. It's not good for them emotionally or health-wise to have that constant stress.'

Today, the groups work well together most of the time. Key to the success of Chris's 'project' was getting the team leaders to work cohesively. 'If they are working together, it just flows.' Along the way that led to one of the leaders stepping down from his role – he had been promoted too quickly and wasn't ready to take on the pressure of leadership, and this reflected in his dealings with the other groups.

Chris places a lot of value on the integrity of his team as a whole. He is scrupulous about fairness, openness, sharing information and being inclusive. Before making promises to a customer – around a deadline, for instance – he seeks the input of the engineers who'll be responsible for meeting that deadline. This keeps him from making promises he can't keep to the customers, while also involving his staff in the process. The feedback Chris has received from his staff reflects this: that he empowers people, 'not that I am overpowering, but give them space, give them room to explore what they need to do.'

When we look at these examples of integrity in action, it is clear that our leaders all have a clear sense of right and wrong and place significant value in maintaining a distinction between these. They are happy to have themselves tested and judged, but they expect the same of those they lead. What is significant is the way they go about instilling the value of integrity into others: with *courage* and *balance*. They are not draconian about it; rather, they are assiduously fair. They are not dramatic about it; rather they display a measured firmness. It starts to become clear how closely linked *courage, balance* and *integrity* are as attributes of emotionally healthy leadership.

Genuine connection

The appointment of Chris to the role of operations manager saw him promoted ahead of the existing production manager, who was an engineer and one of the company's long-term employees. The employee was quite knocked around by this – 'His job had kind of become everything about him' – and ended up taking a couple of months off to come to terms with the situation.

When the engineer returned to work, Chris sat down with him in his office. 'The thing that stood out for me was that he expressed his absolute support for me, even though he felt like I'd got the role that he thought he should have had. His support has continued and that is a real credit to him.'

But this is the thing about Chris. While the engineer displayed high emotional health himself by not holding a grudge, the fact that

Chris is who he is made doing so a lot easier. Chris is, simply, a nice person. He has a seemingly innate ability to genuinely connect with others. His emotional radar is strong, and he sees enormous value in having healthy relationships. When he discusses his background, it is the relationships that often come to the fore: the relationship with his boss, for instance ('That's the reason why I'm sitting here'), and with his family ('I get a feeling of belonging by having connections with my brother, sisters, nieces and nephews'). And when he discusses his work he likes to share stories of heart-to-heart chats with individuals he has sensed are struggling for one reason or other.

After his parents separated, Chris made a point of reaching out to his father (who had moved out). 'I made sure I kept in touch with him. I wanted to remind him that he had a reason to be around.' They continue to have a strong and meaningful relationship.

Graeme feels he has always had an intuitive sense of the value of connections and relationships, though he's not sure where it comes from, given both his parents are introverts and generally happy to keep to themselves. His ability to get along with a range of people saw him elected school captain and later, he believes, was something that helped him progress his local council career.

Graeme joined the Shire of Birchip (as it was then) straight out of school at the age of 18. The population of the shire was about 1100 people and the full-time administrative staff numbered just four: the shire secretary, shire engineer, secretary and junior administrative officer (Graeme's role). 'I had to pretty quickly develop an understanding of how to relate to a broad range of people, from the guys who managed the gardens right through to me and beyond.'

He remembers the shire engineer being a big influence. 'He was well into his fifties, and he had a really good way of dealing with people. He was always respectful but firm and people had a lot of respect for him because he demonstrated that he was there for the best interest of the community. He had a really good way about him in terms of dealing with people.'

Graeme now leads a council with as many employees as there were people living in the entire Shire of Birchip when he was in that first job. But those early lessons have stayed with him, and are no less important now than they have ever been. 'In all my years as a CEO, the importance of understanding how and why relationships work has been critical.'

Of our three leaders, Karenza is the only one who works in an organisation with a specifically compassionate purpose: assisting prisoners to re-establish themselves in mainstream society after their release. It is not hard to see an association between her passion for this work and her own journey from society's 'fringe'.

'It doesn't matter where people have come from and what's happened in their lives, everyone has the potential to be anything that they want. They need to be given the opportunities and the chances … it's too easy to sit back and go, "Ah, they are all losers", or that kind of stuff. That's actually not the case because there, but for the grace of God, go I.'

But while compassion for the disadvantaged is second nature to Karenza, building genuine connections and relationships in her leadership roles has required some effort. For some time, including in her first CEO role, she struggled in this area. 'The eye opener for me was obtaining that first CEO role at 35 – I had set a goal for myself to do it by 40 – and discovering that it was the loneliest job I had ever had.'

The two things that have helped Karenza make stronger connections have been development of her own self-belief – the preparedness to back herself – and the willingness to expose her vulnerabilities, which we described earlier. In particular, her connection with her two senior managers is both strong and genuine, to the point where they are now willing to take risks and share their emotional vulnerabilities with her.

On another level Karenza has learnt that she needs to constantly monitor her connections with others as she goes about developing her ideas. She has a lot of ideas, and moves through them quickly. 'I will have people on board with me, but I go from nought to 100 very quickly and if I keep going I find that I've left everyone too far behind me. So it's about understanding the point that I need to stop and reflect, to look back and check that everyone is still with me.'

And then there are the connections with her organisation's clients.

'We cooked a barbecue for the clients at Christmas. I said to my managers, "No-one else cooks this, we cook this". I set the barbecue on fire, which the clients thought was hilarious. But actions say so much more and I would do the same for the staff. We sit down; we take the time; we say thank you.'

There is no-one right way of genuinely connecting, but what stands out in our three leaders is their *consciousness* of the great benefits of connection, and their willingness to achieve it. For Chris and Graeme this seems to have come fairly readily, from an early age. Karenza, as a leader, has had to learn the hard way, to some extent. That said, there has been no shortage of compassion on Karenza's part – it is compassion and understanding wrought by her own experiences that have underpinned her career from the start.

Adaptability

If there is one thing that stands out as common to our three leaders' stories, it is their early accession into leadership roles. Each of them was recognised as a potential leader at a young age. Each of them has succeeded in leadership, in their own way, with a blend of adaptability and persistence.

Graeme spent the first five years of his career at Birchip. 'I had fantastic exposure to a whole range of council activities, as well as direct exposure to the elected councillors. So I got the full gamut of experience right from day one.'

After five years Graeme moved to the larger Shire of Yarrawonga as its accountant. Not long afterwards, the shire decided to introduce a unitary management structure in which a CEO would have overall responsibility for the administration. (This is the most common structure in local councils today, but was unusual at the time.) At the age of just 26, Graeme was invited to take on that CEO role. 'I was the second-youngest person on the staff, yet they didn't even advertise. They just sidled up to me one day and asked if I would like the job.'

Clearly there was a self-assurance and capability in Graeme that was recognised by the council of the day, and their confidence was well placed. Graeme has continued in CEO roles, adapting to larger and larger councils, for 25 years.

As we have seen, Graeme's preferred approach to dealing with whatever is going on around him is to remain balanced, measured and calm. But he also believes that, at times, he needs to adapt that style in order to achieve a goal.

Not long after taking on his current role, Graeme invested in a leadership development program for his executive team, with a view to developing the sort of authentic leadership culture he was looking for. 'A very short period into that program, I started receiving complaints from the team. They were couched in terms of "We don't like the facilitator's delivery style", but I knew that the real issue was they didn't like the message they were hearing. I've really only had one 'hissy fit' since I came here, and this was it.' In this situation, Graeme chose to keep a firm focus on the fact that the precise reason why they were doing this development work was a reticence on the part of the team to hear difficult messages and understand themselves better, individually and as a group. It worked. 'That was probably a turning point in terms of our evolution here.'

Adapting her approach to the circumstances is something that Karenza finds herself doing quite often. Hers is a world in which success is dependent on the support and sponsorship of a number of external individuals and agencies – especially bureaucrats – and Karenza is acutely aware of the type of impact she needs to have in order to get results.

In a typical meeting with public servants, Karenza takes other people from her team with her, who she knows will offset her exuberance and passion 'and give a sense of stability, safety and calmness'. She will dress conservatively and play calming music on the way to the meeting. 'I might even go and box on that morning to get all the excitement out of me.'

At an international drug treatment conference recently, Karenza presented a workshop with a group of her staff. The audience were largely in jeans and t-shirts, as were her staff, but Karenza wore 'a gorgeous black dress'. In this instance she felt it was important to convey absolute credibility and a strong sense of authority. In contrast, when she visits one of her organisation's residential facilities (providing accommodation for former prisoners) she will wear jeans and a t-shirt herself.

Karenza also sees some limitations to this sort of adaptation. For a start, 'external' adaptation (via choice of clothes and/or language) only works when it is supported by a complementary intent. The politician doesn't become 'one of the people' just by losing his tie; the plainclothes policewoman won't blend into the crowd simply by putting on civilian clothes.

Sometimes, too, it's important to retain some of your 'true' self. Karenza remembers the interview she went through for her current job. 'I really, really wanted the job.' She knew that the interviewers were likely to be conservative and that she needed to avoid being too 'out there'. But she also knew that she needed to 'show the flavour of who I am – the innovation, the cutting edge, the fact that I lead from the heart'. So she tried to find a balance, and it worked. 'In the end it was the passion that got me the job.' It was a powerful lesson in holding on to who she is.

After finishing his business degree, Chris knew where he could adapt and where he needed not to compromise in order to remain happy. He is a country boy and, although there were many more job opportunities on offer in Melbourne, he knew instinctively that he needed to stay in the country. 'The city just didn't appeal to me.'

But his first job was in sales, which was also out of his comfort zone. 'I remember when I was back at school being petrified of getting up in front of the class and talking', yet now he was required to stand up in front of groups of sales dealers and teach them about his products. He also had to spend day after day on the telephone, talking to people and drumming up interest in the products. 'At the end of the day your head is just mush, because you've put out so much information. I used to wonder how it was possible that I had done it.'

There is a competitive streak to Chris, which no doubt helped push him through these challenges. 'Always having something to aim for has been important.' Whether it is overcoming his fears in that first role, or dealing with his ongoing back injury, 'I just have this inner belief that I won't cave in – I won't give in to it.'

Since being promoted into his operations management role, Chris continues to think and to question himself and his actions. He wants to get the most out of himself. He is not afraid of seeking feedback and tries to gauge as honestly as he can how well he is going as a leader. 'Part of it is just having an open door and having people come in. Sometimes it is directly asking people about what they see and are experiencing.' Like Graeme and Karenza, Chris sees benefit in occasionally stepping outside his 'normal' personality. 'I think sometimes actually letting a bit of emotion out and letting people see some frustration can be useful.'

While all our leaders have a strong drive to succeed, there is a strong sense that they see the onus being on themselves to make that happen. They believe that effective leadership requires them to adapt to circumstances – forcing or bullying their way to the top is not an option. Again, consciousness plays an important role here; they are highly tuned in to how they are being received and, more importantly, the connection between the way they come across and how they get results.

Authenticity

After falling short of her own expectations in her first CEO role, Karenza decided to be more honest about how she saw herself. 'What that experience really taught me to do all the time is hold up a mirror and seek feedback. I didn't do that in that [first] role because I wouldn't have wanted to see the reflection. Later I understood that sometimes you need to look in that mirror and go "Wow ... okay ... wow! Is that true?"'

Today Karenza is single minded about hearing feedback that might be uncomfortable – about hearing the things she doesn't really want to hear. Her drive is for her organisation to be successful in what it does and to make a difference in the world – and if that means confronting an uncomfortable truth from time to time, she's happy to pay that price. In her view, her organisation can't succeed in the long term if her leaders, and particularly she herself, can't express themselves authentically.

Most people who meet Karenza would be surprised to learn that she has been contending with an eating disorder for many years. Like most eating disorders, Karenza's condition cannot be said to have been beaten even if there are no current symptoms –

completely overcoming such a disorder takes time.

What stands out in Karenza's case is the way she has been able to come to terms with her disorder as one aspect of her personality, but not allow it to prevent her from building a successful career. In a similar vein, as we have already mentioned, Karenza maintains a strong desire to be 'the best', while recognising that being the best is no longer essential to her fulfilment. She has a strong desire to be unique, but has developed an understanding within herself that fighting for uniqueness is counterproductive if it means losing sight of a broader view of what actually needs to get done.

'I think in the past I would beat myself up about stuff that I had fallen short of. There was a bar that I would set myself, and I would brood. "This isn't good enough and you're not good enough, and how can you even be in this job?" Changing that by understanding more about myself, those distortion filters and saying, "That's not true. What's really happened here? Let's look at this differently. You have actually done X and Y and Z, how does that feel? It actually feels okay".'

There is a quiet authenticity to Chris when he discusses himself as a leader. In the past his leadership potential seems to have been recognised by others before he saw it himself. As a young footballer he eventually became his team's assistant coach. 'The coach said to me once, "You don't say much, but when you do say something, it's got a really strong point".' But something held him back; he didn't quite see himself as fitting into the group or the culture. 'I wouldn't have considered myself a leader as much then because I reflect that I wasn't necessarily comfortable leading in that football environment.'

Chris has a simple measure of his own authenticity: the extent to which he feels 'more like himself' when he is at work. Today he is comfortable accepting that most of the time these days he can 'just feel the same whether I am at home or at work. If I go back four or five years, that was definitely not the case – people who knew me at work and out of work could see the difference'.

Chris operates in a reinforcing circle of self-belief. 'When I'm feeling under pressure or feel down, for whatever reason, I like to acknowledge to myself what I'm capable of – that I am actually quite capable of doing certain things. Having those wins, and remembering them …'

Chris seems to gain strength from recognising his particular uniqueness in the context of the wider world around him. He took part in an 'executive forum' in his region, with exposure to leaders in a number of quite different industries from his own, including banking, printing and health. Although one of the youngest in the room, Chris took what he could learn from the experience without feeling overwhelmed or inadequate. He subsequently took part in a community leadership program. Again, he found the exposure to external perspectives both reinforcing and motivating, while not threatening his own authentic expression of himself.

Authenticity also plays out for Chris in his appreciation of nature. It was one of the things that held him back from the idea of moving to the city, where he would have felt anything but authentic. 'I regularly go for hikes and being in the region that I am, there are plenty of places. There are waterfalls and mountains and stuff like that … I love that so much.'

Before Graeme took up his current role, he 'had a perspective that leadership was about having a leadership facade. It was more important you had the professional leadership facade and you should never let it down. When I came here, I quickly learned that they didn't care about the facade. They wanted to drill holes through the facade and actually understand the person.'

So as Graeme worked to change the culture of his new organisation, he also worked on being more authentic himself. Graeme is clearly proud of what he and his team have been able to achieve, and the strength of the organisation that has been built around him. However, there is no boastfulness. Rather, there is the hope that others might learn from his council's successes, and a recognition that there is always more to learn. 'It's okay to be good at what we do.'

'Our city is often seen as a fairly highly effective and performing organisation. We have something to share so we encourage people to actively participate in sector opportunities and contribute to the sector. They are also a really good opportunity for people to learn from others, to get out of the organisation and understand what's also happening in the broader world.'

Graeme is sensitive to the need to bring others along with him, and in particular to have those who are new to his team understanding where he and the rest of his management group have come from.

'We're a bus that is going down the road and at several stops people get on and off. What we sometimes underestimate is that some of the people that are on the bus only got on at the second-last stop. They have missed the journey, or the early part of the journey. So we have to reinvest so that everyone is at the same point on the journey.'

It is rare to see a combination of deep understanding – and ongoing questioning – of self with authenticity, humility and a minimum of self-absorption. Each of our leaders has moved past the need for excessive introspection while maintaining sufficient inner questioning to avoid arrogance. They all spend a lot of their time being real and genuine – presenting who they really are.

Synthesis

'Recently I sat down in one of our houses and just drank cups of tea with five sex offenders. I just sat there and listened to their lives and where they were at and what's happening and what was important to them, and the connection to our business. I understand more the context of what's happening when people are talking about their issues and challenges.'

The decisions that Karenza and her staff make can literally be life and death, given the sensitivity of the situations some of their clients find themselves in. So for Karenza, a detailed understanding has been important from the beginning.

'I think for me, understanding every aspect and element of the business so I understood every role – the cogs in the wheel, how they all turned and worked – meant I could make better decisions. When I first came, I did every role in the organisation for my first 90 days. I wanted to understand every function of my business, every commitment each person was making. I wanted to see what that was like.'

Maintaining this broad perspective and understanding the impact and influence of the component parts of the business is critical to its success and Karenza is very aware of her role in leading this. She is also aware of her tendency to get 'caught in the drama'; retaining a fully rounded understanding of what is going on inside her organisation and, particularly, with the clients, is one of the ways she manages this. 'If I get lost in a mountain of paperwork and bureaucracy and conversations with commissioners, I won't know what the hell I am talking about if I don't connect back with our clients.'

On starting his current role, Graeme also set out to gain as thorough an understanding as he could of its context. 'I set about trying to deeply understand what was the culture of the municipality, what made it a great place, what makes it up, what is its core, what are its values.'

With a number of local government CEO roles behind him, Graeme had a clear vision of the type of leadership he wanted to develop among his team, and from his research he was able to isolate the areas of weakness in the existing structure. There was that culture of 'cordial hypocrisy' we mentioned earlier, with some people agreeing on a course of action when they met as an executive team, 'but then going and doing or saying, either openly or covertly, something very different'. This initially hampered his efforts to achieve the organisational culture he desired. 'Any variation between words and actions is magnified further into the organisation.' Over time, Graeme was able to build a team around him who understood his desire for a more authentic leadership and operated with more emotional awareness.

Graeme is clear that he needs to continue to understand and explore the complexities and needs of the municipality and its changing population. He is also clear that the organisation needs to synthesise the data and information it continually receives (both internal and external) to excel at what it does.

Chris believes his original appointment to the operations management role was in part due to the capacity of some of the directors to identify and nurture ability in others. He believes he has developed some of the same capability. 'That's been the next step of my growth, being able to do that.

'We tried to bring a guy in to look after the factory entirely [as a supervisor] but it didn't work.' Now there are three people sharing that role, and reporting to Chris. 'We needed to understand all the parts of the business and how they work together to come to this point. It is now working and we have developed those guys and they communicate well.'

'One of the guys – I don't think his upbringing was all that good; I don't think he was that confident – was an angry young guy, but after his apprenticeship we made him one of those team leaders. I have watched his growth and he's developed brilliantly.' He's not completely there yet, and still needs some coaching, but Chris is sure he was able to pick a good person for the job, even if it wasn't obvious at the start. 'We just saw something in him, and you take little steps and you see a little bit more.'

Chris identifies that 'seeing something in others' is more than a hunch or a feeling. He has always watched for not only what is demonstrated or said by others but also the reactions and responses of others (the impact) in that situation. Even in his football coaching days, he saw potential in others – not just in their match skills, but also through the way in which they engaged on and off the field.

All our leaders have developed the capacity to notice what is in their environment, to listen – not only to what is being said, but also what is *not* being said – and to bring their own knowledge and understanding into the mix and then find the best way of moving forward. They do so in their own ways, but each of these leaders has the ability to synthesise information and situations to achieve the best results.

Continuity

Manufacturing in today's Australia is an industry under pressure, with announcements of factory closures and job losses making regular appearances on evening news bulletins. This can put employees of any manufacturing business on edge from time to time, with bad news a risk to morale.

So when Chris's boss, one of the owners of the business, addresses a monthly meeting of all staff and starts talking openly about 'it being very quiet at the moment', Chris will assess the mood and, if necessary, take action to quietly wrap up the conversation. It's not about protecting people from bad news, but rather managing the risk that bad news 'on the margins' can easily be exaggerated, in the minds of already nervous people, into a major concern. And of course the last thing Chris or the business needs is a fall-off in productivity during a lull in sales.

Chris spends a lot of his time managing risks of various sorts that could threaten the continuity that keeps a business like his running smoothly and profitably.

A common scenario is balancing the sometimes rapidly changing demands of customers with the need to keep the factory running to plan, with minimum interruption. When a sales representative occasionally yields to a customer request that will require what Chris sees as unreasonable disruption to the factory, he is comfortable saying 'No'. He feels that the risk of annoying a customer will be offset by the benefits of maintaining continuity in the factory (and potentially satisfying a different customer or customers down the track). There are other situations where some disruption is warranted and, again, Chris is willing to talk and explain – this time to, say, a disgruntled engineer – in order to keep things moving.

In both these scenarios the thing that stands out is that Chris is sure enough in himself that he is able to weigh up and take calculated risks. He is neither overly cautious nor impulsive. He simply keeps his eye on the goal of keeping things moving.

Another area in which Chris promotes continuity is in his ongoing efforts to build a strong and confident team around him. For instance, Chris has developed his team leaders – none of whom had leadership experience initially – to a point where he is now comfortable leaving the factory to run without him for a few days, knowing that everything will continue as it should. 'They can't just rely on me being there', and they don't – his team leaders are confident and competent enough to operate autonomously. But again, one senses that this has been part of the plan – that Chris is balancing risk and reward in the amount of autonomy he is willing to distribute.

Graeme links the concept of consistency when talking about continuity within his organisation.

'I think if you become irrational because you are emotional, I think you do lose that degree of consistency and people then start to question whether they can trust that you are going to be the same one day as the next ... If you are going to sustain a leadership approach, you have got to be living what you stand for 24/7.'

When he raises it, it is normally in conjunction with his strongest theme – one we've mentioned before – of robust values. For Graeme, consistency of values is a way of mitigating the risk of disruption and maintaining continuity.

The recruitment process is a good example. A big part of ensuring continuity comes down to recruiting the right people, then nurturing them in line with a desired culture. Of course every recruitment exercise has an associated risk attached to it. It is always possible to employ the wrong person, and that can cause problems. 'My sense is that you only need one or two who don't fit for that to cause a major disruption.' And indeed a recent experience reinforced this, when a new manager was recruited who didn't work out. 'He constantly challenged, constantly questioned, constantly referred to "When I did it in my previous organisation we did it this way ...". It was just this constant banter.' There was no let up.

The flip side of that risk is that you recruit too conservatively – 'that we just recruit clones, and that's not healthy either'.

Graeme gets a lot of fulfilment from taking a risk with people and giving them a chance to develop, 'not only in their work life, but as people. At the end of the day my job I think is to create an opportunity and allow people to grow both as individuals, as healthy people and in their work. If I can create an environment and continue to support them to do that, we will deliver great outcomes here and they will be great people'.

Building a stable, motivated team to ensure continuity and consistency in the organisation is a strong theme of Karenza's too. However, in her case giving people 'rope' to achieve this is something she has probably had to learn to do, and learn the value of, more than our other two leaders.

'I used to believe that you could do it on your own. I used to believe that as long as I am at the top, if they can't do it, I will fix it.'

Karenza tells of a recent situation in which a tender needed rewriting before submission the next day. 'In the past I would have gone, "Right, get this guy here, get her there, pull them all in ... and no-one leaves tonight until this tender is rewritten." And then I would have said that it wasn't good enough and gone and done it myself anyway.'

This time, one of Karenza's young leaders – someone with a reputation in the past of being highly cynical about leading in the business – took charge. 'She facilitated and ran the session, and she ripped the tender apart. She pointed to which bits were missing; she pointed out what needed to be done to get ahead of the competitors.

I just sat there in stunned amazement, then left them to it. What was fascinating was for me to have the confidence to do that – to walk away and leave them to it. I was just beaming from ear to ear.' Once again there was risk here: without overseeing every aspect the tender document could have fallen short of Karenza's expectations. However, the development of two people came into play: first, that of the young leader, in whom Karenza could sense newfound confidence. And second, that of Karenza herself, who could see that allowing this leader to run with the project, and in so doing building her confidence still further, would be highly beneficial to the organisation in terms of building continuity and increasing its resilience.

In Karenza's eyes, having gained the ability to develop and nurture the people working for her means that 'I am actually now leading. Before I would just go, "Oh, just give it to me and I'll do it". Now I have a significantly greater awareness of not doing that'. What Karenza has realised is that this is actually better for the continuity of the business and the things she wants to achieve and develop.

In those last comments, Karenza pins down a strong theme of leadership portrayed by all our leaders. It is the sense of moving away from reactivity towards a steady proactivity in the way they manage risk in the business – it is the leader as conductor rather than fire fighter.

Each of our leaders is creating a working environment that has a rhythm and continuity to it, as opposed to lurching from crisis to crisis. They have all removed the need to personally be involved in solving every problem. They are doing this by building the ability of others to recognise what decisions and actions will be consistent with their organisation's values and direction, and therefore to take the calculated risks necessary to maintain continuity.

Seeing potential

Karenza learnt a thing or two about seeing future possibilities in her life out of her father's transition from almost-prisoner to the navy, and from her own escape from drugs. 'Understanding that change can happen because people believe in you, or you believe in you.'

As a leader, she learnt more still from the situation of her first CEO role – particularly the aftermath of its not working out as well as it could.

'I learned that you must back yourself, trust yourself, and believe in yourself. The judgement that I made earlier on was actually the right judgement, but I didn't act on it. Trying to understand why I hadn't acted on it was really quite significant and important.'

Through the changes she has made in her life and career, Karenza has been able to envision possibility and act on it, even if she did not necessarily understand that this was happening at the time. Seeing her own potential and the possibilities it brings as a result is something she now appreciates. 'I think when I began to have some of that self-belief, when I began to think maybe I am good at this, maybe this is okay ... then I was able to lift myself.'

We often associate the word 'visionary' with something external to an individual – with the future state of an organisation or community. Karenza demonstrates that vision can be as much about seeing potential in yourself.

The biggest test of Chris's enthusiasm for life and his own potential came after his short-lived marriage ended.

'I got married and before the end of the year I was divorced; I was on my own. So I went from being married and feeling secure and everything, to all of a sudden it's all thrown up in the air. I also quit football that year. That was pretty tough for me because I had been doing that for 10 years, so every weekend I knew what I was doing. So that finished and then within a month my relationship was over as well.'

All of those situations that Chris had envisioned for himself were no longer there.

Perhaps he had learnt from watching a decline in his dad's health after his parents' separation, but Chris's response to his own situation was to take up running. Physical activity helped him to see a way past a lonely and unhappy time in his life. 'I'd leave work and go to a mate's place and we'd run 10 or 15 kilometres. I can still picture where I was and how I felt ... the endorphins and the adrenaline that was going through my body because of the physical activity, and how much better I felt. I can still remember it today. That was a good thing for me.'

On the organisational side, Chris doesn't necessarily find it easy to envision the future or imagine the possibilities and potential for both himself and the business. However, his boss, one of the owners of the business, has made this a focus for their conversations and Chris embraces these challenges with enthusiasm. 'He challenges me all the time, but in the right way.' Chris has learnt to explore and imagine what is possible – to understand that this is critical for the business in terms of exploring boundaries and developing new markets.

Chris has also been given the opportunity to better understand the qualities and capabilities he brings to a situation (his own potential) through the positions he has been offered within the business.

Graeme's first lesson in seeing potential probably came from his careers teacher, who saw this in him while he was at school. It was that teacher who suggested he apply for the junior job with the local shire council out of school. From there he had an opportunity to get involved in most aspects of the administration of local government: from taking minutes in council meetings to organising home help to issuing building permits. 'I actually issued a building permit to the Russell Street bombers!'

Today, with his current team, Graeme has an interesting take on potential.

On one hand, to maintain the organisation's strategic direction and achieve its vision, he believes there is plenty of potential still to be tapped – not only among his management team but among all the staff. His team has been working on building engagement, because of a recognised correlation between how engaged someone feels and their level of discretionary effort. 'There is some evidence to suggest that up to 65 per cent of any organisation's productivity comes from discretionary effort.'

On the other hand, Graeme is conscious that 'We are not built physically or psychologically to run a constant marathon'. So he keeps the sustainability and resilience of his leadership team on his mind. 'We started to plan, particularly as an executive team, around what we personally need to do: "How am I going to take responsibility to ensure that I can sustain my level of leadership resilience over a long term?".'

Graeme identifies that realising organisational potential and maximising discretionary effort also requires leaders in the business to hold a strong and positive vision of the future. They need to see what is possible and then be able to engage others in understanding and implementing the steps to achieve this. He believes these qualities can be developed and strengthened in his people through the work they are undertaking.

Visionary, enthusiastic and positive about the future; resilient and adaptable. These are all descriptions of the 'potential' of our three leaders. There is both a sense of not allowing setbacks to linger and of being optimistic about the future, but also of not taking the future for granted. And of course there is what has been clear through all that we have shared so far: the quiet confidence that these leaders have in themselves and their own potential.

Part 2: Understanding Emotional Health

So, what thoughts came to mind as you read about our three leaders? Notwithstanding the reality that they are three quite different people, are there qualities and characteristics they possess between them that reflect the type of leader you would like to work for? Can you see in them aspects of the type of leadership that you aspire to show yourself? Did you recognise characteristics that these leaders share with those who have been sitting quietly in the corner of that room in your mind from the start of this book?

You may feel that emotionally healthy leadership is still a blurry concept, that it is quite hard to pin down. That would be entirely excusable, but we ask you to bear with us. The nature of emotional health is that it is difficult to 'draw' with hard edges. Understanding it requires a degree of what we call 'allowing': a willingness to continue along the journey without being entirely sure what you will find when you get there. The portrait we have offered only represents the first section of the path towards understanding emotionally healthy leadership. Now we can start on the next part of our exploration.

There is one other point to make before we move on. It's possible that you may feel a little daunted by the style of leadership we have been describing so far. If that's the case, please don't be. Our leaders would be the first to admit that they are not perfect – that they still have a lot to learn and a long way to go. (That admission, paradoxically, is one of the things that indicates higher levels of emotional health.) What they have learnt to be is highly conscious of themselves – their thoughts, their behaviours and the impact they have on others – and to recognise and overcome the various influences and constraints that they experience, either from others or themselves.

It is our belief that almost anyone can do that, with the right combination of understanding and choice. Let us explain.

Choosing your responses

We can look at the concept of emotional health from a number of different but interrelated perspectives. Let's start with a notion that most people find fairly easy to grasp: the 'line of choice'.

Imagine you are in the car, driving along happily, when from out of nowhere someone cuts dangerously in front of you. You are forced to brake quickly to avoid an accident. How would you react? If you are like most people you would probably react in one of the traditional ways: a heavy hand on the horn, a tirade of abuse, the flashing of headlights, or all three of the above.

This typical reaction to a typical situation is a classic example of what we call an 'automatic response'. It is a 'default' behaviour: we don't consciously think about honking, swearing or flashing our headlights – we just do it.

Now think about how, at some time in the past, you've approached a conversation about your performance with a manager you didn't get along with. Or a time in your school days when a teacher commented on a poor piece of work. Or a time at home when your partner criticised you for, say, not pulling your weight. Try to really take yourself back to that discussion and relive it in your mind.

How did the discussion start? Did you go into it with an open mind or were you on the defensive from the word go? Did you find yourself fairly quickly justifying yourself, regardless of what the manager/teacher/partner said? Most of us have been in this situation at some stage and, if we're honest, most of us have had defensive moments.

What is happening in this situation is very similar to what is happening in the 'car braking' scenario. The difference in the workplace, at school and at home is that instead of horn-honking, our automatic response to being challenged or criticised is defensiveness, denial, blame or justification.

In all these cases there's a good chance that, on later reflection, you recognised that your behaviour was ultimately unnecessary and unhelpful and probably not the best choice you could have made at the time. You realised that abusing another driver from within your own vehicle does little but raise your own blood pressure, and that being cut off didn't actually delay you in any case. You realised that starting a conversation from a defensive perspective was never going to lead to an open discussion – and that perhaps some of the criticism could have been relevant anyway.

You allowed yourself this reflection, and then left it at that ... until the next time.

Perhaps once in a while after situations like this you have gone on to wonder whether it is really possible to avoid angry or defensive responses. After all, the responses are automatic, aren't they?

The truth is that it *is* possible to change your responses to situations like these. It *is* possible to react with more conscious thought; it *is* possible to think rationally – as you did on reflection – in the moment of the situation and not just afterwards. Learning to do so has a lot to do with increasing emotional health.

Let's have a look at what is going on here.

In our work we draw a line – the 'line of choice' – between automatic responses to challenging situations, along the lines of what we've been describing (typically denial, blame, justification or defensiveness), and the more emotionally healthy option of a thoughtful and constructive response to those situations (see Figure 1). When we choose the latter option we are consciously taking personal responsibility – not for the situation itself, but for the way we react to it.

We say that automatic responses are 'below the line' while the alternatives – constructive, thoughtful responses – are 'above the line'.

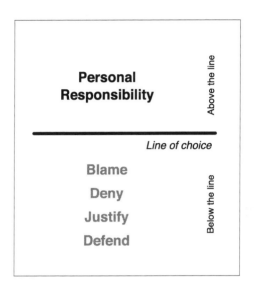

Figure 1: The Line of Choice (adapted from the work of Robert Kiyosaki).

Notice that we use the word 'choice' here. For ultimately there is a personal choice to be made between operating above or below the line, even though it may not feel like it as our hand hits the horn or the excuses start flowing.

Making that choice requires the sort of clear thinking we described earlier. In other words, it requires us to be present in the moment. Achieving this in everyday situations takes both training and practice, especially when you consider that making the choice has to be done very quickly – American psychotherapist and author Tara Bennett-Goleman calls the space between impulse and action the 'magic quarter second'. Some of that training and practice we get from life in general. As we 'grow up', we tend to learn to take more personal responsibility than we did when we were young. In practice, however, the vast majority of us only take personal responsibility for our behaviour and our responses some of the time, even as adults. At other times – when that other driver cuts us off, for instance – we slip below the line quite easily.

Spending some time below the line – blaming, denying, defending and justifying – might seem quite normal to us. The challenge is to increase your awareness of these responses and, over time, to choose healthier ones more often. In other words, to constantly increase the amount of time you spend being present and 'above the line'. Achieving this requires a high level of awareness about yourself and the way you see your interactions with others.

There are many sources of emotional triggers – circumstances that elicit an above- or below-the-line response. Let's have a look at two simple, everyday situations by way of example.

First, imagine yourself coming across a piece of waste paper or other litter in a park. A typical automated response to seeing this would be to feel angry at whoever it was who dropped litter in the park. A healthier, and less stressful, response would be to pause and reflect on the situation. Have a look around. Perhaps the area has become a dumping ground and the person who left this rubbish was simply following the lead of others. Or maybe there are no bins in the area: perhaps this litter is a sign of someone's frustration at a lack of services.

Either way, the question could be asked: 'What can I do?' Can you contact the local council? Can you write to the newspaper? Can you simply lead by example and recommit to making sure you take your own waste away? Any of these responses would be more positive – more 'above the line' – than simply getting angry.

Another situation you may be familiar with is arriving first thing at work to find the communal kitchen full of dirty cups and glasses from the day before.

A raw, angry and frustrated reaction to the mess – potentially including a few 'words' directed at whoever happens to be in hearing range – would be a typical below-the-line response to the situation.

An above-the-line response would be to pause before reacting and take the time to see the situation and its consequences from other points of view. No matter what the state of the kitchen, you still have a choice about how to react to it, and pausing to reflect will allow the options to become available to you.

One option might be to do nothing – to accept that communal kitchens have always been this way and probably always will be, and you don't need to take personal ownership of the mess.

Another option might be to tidy the kitchen up – again – though this choice comes with the obvious risk that others will fail to appreciate your efforts, which might just escalate your frustrations when the situation repeats itself a few days later.

Yet another option could be to try talking with the other staff. There are still more choices here. You could share your feelings ('I am feeling disappointed …'), discuss the need for compromise because you all work together ('What can we do that will work for all of us?') or seek out different perspectives – making a genuine effort to listen.

The point here is that there are many other ways of responding to a situation like a messy kitchen, and most of the alternatives to getting angry and frustrated would be more 'above the line' than the automatic one, that is, they would involve taking more personal responsibility for your *reaction* (while not accepting personal responsibility for the *situation*).

# # #

If you think back to our portrait of emotionally healthy leadership, perhaps you can recall some examples of how our leaders described reflecting before acting, and consciously chose to remain 'above the line'.

One example relates to the situation Chris found himself in when a director of the company walked onto the factory floor without the correct safety equipment. Chris could have ignored it, given that the person was senior to him, then perhaps later vented his frustrations to another colleague or to a friend outside work. But that wouldn't have changed anything except his level of stress. He could have confronted the director in the factory in front of the employees, but that would probably have embarrassed the director and even, in the longer term, potentially limited Chris's career. What Chris did do was reflect before he acted. He then took the director aside and quietly explained why disregarding the safety rules was problematic. There was no blaming or anger involved. Chris chose, as he often does, to operate 'above the line'.

Another example was the situation Karenza found herself in in her first CEO role, with a general manager who she could neither work with nor change. There were plenty of potential below-the-line responses, and for a while Karenza admits that she fell into some of these, including blaming the general manager for what was occurring, and becoming increasingly frustrated. However, in the end Karenza took personal responsibility for the situation and chose to leave the role and the organisation. In her current role she is far more conscious of her reactions and will step in to provide constructive feedback and coaching to improve performance as an alternative to blame and frustration. She is able to stay 'above the line' more and more often.

Understanding this idea of operating above or below the line is the first step towards understanding the concept of emotional health. Let's now look at another perspective.

The centres of intelligence

If you were asked by someone to describe what you 'think' with, you'd probably look at them strangely and respond with 'My brain, of course'. Interestingly, it is not as simple as that. In fact, when we are *effectively* thinking we are doing so not just with our brain but with our *whole body*.

In this information era, most people's thoughts operate a bit like Twitter or Facebook: a never-ending stream of notes, recollections, to dos, ideas and inspirations. Time moves quickly as the mind flutters from one thought to the next. If you've ever had a day that you looked back on and wondered where it went, wondered why you can hardly remember what happened, you know what we are talking about.

As leaders, this kind of thinking can cause you to be less than effective in your role – particularly in the ways in which you focus on what is important, engage and enable others, and work to achieve what is expected.

When you are surrounded by clutter (either physical or mental), it is hard to see the organisation and the world around you with clarity. More significantly, this clutter forces a sort of rapid-fire thinking. This thinking is inherently biased and fails to consider the full set of possibilities and ramifications.

Our reading in ancient eastern philosophy teaches us that clear, effective thinking is achieved using a balance of the three 'centres of intelligence': the body or 'gut', heart and head (Figure 2). This notion is supported by modern neuroscience, in particular the work of Antonio Damasio.[1]

---

[1] See Antonio Damasio, *Descartes' Error: Emotion, Reason, and the Human Brain*, Putnam Publishing, 1994.

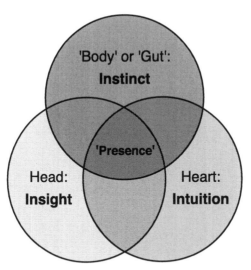

Figure 2: The centres of intelligence

Put very simply: 'body thinking' is thinking based on 'gut knowing' – what we often call *instinct*; 'heart thinking' is thinking based on feelings – what we often call *intuition*; and 'head thinking' is thinking based on interpretation and analysis – what we often call *insight*.

You might argue that instinct, intuition and insight are all pretty much the same, and in fact some dictionaries do list instinct and intuition as synonyms. However, we ask you to stay with us here. Looked at holistically, there is a subtlety to the difference between the three centres that we feel is intrinsic in these words – a subtlety that should become clear as we explore them.

We are all capable of thinking in all three of these ways. However, in our own development process as we learn to cope with the world, we tend to lean more strongly towards one of the three, which then becomes our primary filter for perceiving what we think is reality. We develop a tendency to trust the information that comes from our preferred centre over others. Conversely, we find ourselves mistrusting or avoiding what the other centres are telling us. As a result, our thinking is not balanced across the three centres, and it is therefore not as clear and effective as it could be.

You are probably already more familiar with this concept than you may be aware.

Among the people you work with there will be some who are very aware of their immediate environment and *instinctively* sense what response is needed in any given situation. They move into action without requiring a lot of information or concerning themselves about the personal dynamics of the situation. In other words, they react first in an instinctual ('gut knowing') way.

Then there will be those who think through 'feeling' or 'with their heart'. These people have a need to engage and connect with others in order to be appreciated and valued. As they do this, they are highly *intuitive* to others' needs and wants and adapt and adjust their own behaviours in order to meet them.

The third broad group of people you will find are the 'head thinkers': those who prefer to use their thinking to interpret and analyse a situation, then use that *insight* to work out what they believe will be needed. They seek security in the choices they make and using their insight helps them feel prepared to cope with what they anticipate might be ahead.

At first you may find it difficult to distinguish which centre of intelligence you most strongly associate with. However, as you learn more about the centres and practise distinguishing them, you will notice the varying degrees to which you draw on instinct, intuition and insight – and one of these more often than the others – at different times.

To demonstrate how the three centres might play out in practice, imagine you are sitting in a meeting with your team. An issue has come up in relation to a member of the team who has not completed his or her part of a task and the project you are all working on has stalled as a result.

After a long conversation about the impact of this, everyone is starting to look to you, as the leader, to make a decision about what to do next. It is precisely in this sort of pressured environment that we tend to revert to our preferred thinking centre. So you are likely to draw on your own preference first. You will think and act in one of three ways (before considering anything else):

- You will rely on *'gut' feel* – on your *instinct* – to make a call, paying less attention to the facts and feelings of those in the room or those who will be directly affected by the situation. Once a decision is made, it is often final – you will resist going back over old ground.

- You will rely on your *heart* – on your *intuition* – to decide, doing the best you can to weigh up the emotional impact on all of those in the room. Your preference will be to do whatever can be done to avoid upsetting the person who has delayed the project, even if it is clear they have contributed to the situation.

- You will rely on your *head* – on your *insight* – to make a decision using the facts of the situation along with consideration of the outcome and the resulting consequences. Intuition and instinct play a minimal role, as they can bring a little too much 'grey' into the situation. You may procrastinate on taking the next step, just in case there is something you haven't thought about.

It should be clear that each of these scenarios represents a quite distinct perspective on the situation and the way in which different people may respond. It is important to note that your own response may not be so heavily weighted towards one centre, however most people will have an initial preference for one over the others. With increasing emotional health, we become more capable of drawing on all three centres as guides to our responses – something we call 'whole body thinking'. We start to approach a wisdom in leadership that is simultaneously decisive, compassionate and logically coherent.

Whole body thinking

As we said earlier, achieving real clarity in our thinking only occurs when we are able to connect with all three centres. 'Whole body thinking' is thinking that integrates the 'gut', heart and head, regardless of the individual's bias towards one of those.

You will be familiar with this clarity – though perhaps not at work. We often experience it in moments when we are sitting in the sun, walking through a forest or on a beach, playing with our children or literally 'smelling the roses'.

It's thinking with absolute clarity, thinking that cuts through the fog of day-to-day clutter and sees what is in front of us with a whole new perspective. It's 'thinking without thinking'.

Most of us can do this occasionally; some can do it more often – which is where emotional health becomes relevant.

Those with high emotional health are able to integrate the three centres and achieve whole body thinking more often than those with average emotional health, whilst those with low emotional health may not experience it at all.

Just as we require awareness of our responses in order to operate 'above the line' more often, we also need consciousness of our thinking preferences in order to more frequently engage and integrate each of our centres of intelligence. Once again, it is about choice. With consciousness, we are able to 'catch our reactions' and choose to operate above the line; with consciousness, we are able to choose to reconnect with our non-preferred centres and more fully integrate all three centres.

However, there is a subtle but important difference here. Where consciousness of the line of choice can directly lead to a change in behaviour, awareness of the need to integrate the centres of intelligence inspires connection with the non-preferred centres ... which in turn leads to an altered outlook and, potentially, changed behaviour.

An example from one of our leaders might make this clearer.

Karenza's preferred thinking style is heart thinking. 'I feel everything.' Acutely aware of this, Karenza goes to some lengths to ensure she maintains a connection with her 'gut' and head centres.

The best way to connect with the 'gut' is to engage in physical activity: specifically boxing and swimming in Karenza's case. When she is doing these sorts of activity, 'I don't think. Everything stops and it crystallises. It flows and I know that in that time and space and moment ... that's when I'm most emotionally healthy.'

For Karenza, making this connection through activity has an effect on her ability to be 'in the moment' at other times, such as when she is in a meeting or conversation. 'I can go there and I am focused completely on you: on everything that is happening, what you are saying, your body language, all the things that you're telling me and I am really, really listening.'

Karenza describes a situation in which she was aware of being disconnected to her head centre. 'I was in this space and I was aware that my anxieties heightened. This space doesn't feel good. I knew I had to step out of this space. If I connected more with my heart I would tune into the anxiety; I had to connect with my head.' Karenza applied a simple technique for making this connection. 'I lay down and I put my hands on my head – literally my hands on my head –

and I stayed in that space for an hour. I just sat in that space with my hands on my head and said, "Let that go". It was interesting because within an hour I had completely grounded and calmed myself. I had let the anxiety go and I was feeling comfortable and okay. The issue hadn't changed; nothing around me had changed, nothing at all. It was exactly the same, but I had changed.'

Both Graeme and Chris are also aware of the need to maintain connections with their non-preferred centres. They are both head thinkers, so rely on physical activity (running for Graeme, walking for Chris) and opportunities to connect and engage through time with family to reinforce their 'gut' and heart centres respectively.

Karenza's descriptions demonstrate the link between the line of choice and the centres of intelligence. 'I know now that when I feel my anxiety rising, I'm going to start going to automatic responses [below-the-line behaviours]. I will stop engaging and I will stop thinking.' It is at this point of recognition that she will move to reconnect with her non-preferred centres of intelligence. 'Then there are much better decisions, much better choices, much better leadership.'

Leadership distinctions

So far we've looked at two separate but interrelated perspectives of emotionally healthy leadership: personal responsibility guided by the 'line of choice' and whole body thinking through the 'centres of intelligence'. While these concepts are highly relevant to emotional health in a leadership context, they also pertain to each of us as individuals and to the way we observe and interact with the world around us.

We'll now explore a third perspective of emotional health, one that pertains specifically to leadership.

As we built up our portrait of an emotionally healthy leader, we were able to distinguish nine attributes shared by our leaders. We believe that the ability to combine and embrace these as a whole goes a long way towards defining what it is that separates emotionally healthy leaders from less healthy ones.

These nine distinctions operate in a similar way to the centres of intelligence in that each of us will identify with and/or be drawn towards a small number of them (typically three or four). This selection of distinctions will feel familiar to us – we might even consider them to be our 'strengths'. As our emotional health increases, we will be able to increasingly incorporate the other, less preferred, characteristics into the way we lead (just as we can increasingly integrate the three centres of intelligence).

As you read through the following descriptions of the nine leadership distinctions, reflect first on those you feel are already part of the way you lead and engage others. Some of these behaviours and qualities will just feel part of who you are and have been over the years. Others will be those you have learnt through your career choices and training. Others will reflect the characteristics of important and significant people in your life, while still others may have come to you through the values and principles you hold dear and won't compromise in the way in which you live your life.

Courage – Able to step forward to say or do what is needed with both compassion and directness; meeting the moment with confidence and dealing with what is in front of you constructively and effectively, while also ensuring that others who are involved are supported and engaged.

Balance – In tune and in harmony with all aspects of your environment and yourself; maintaining a calm approach in any situation and creating a sense of unity and inclusion with others; appreciating multiple perspectives as well as holding your own.

Integrity – True to your values and yourself and to those around you; being consistent and transparent in what you see as important and on which you won't compromise, while at the same time respecting that there are other perspectives and alternatives.

Genuine connection – Able to build and maintain strong and enduring relationships through meaningful connections and communication; looking after both yourself and others in a balanced and compassionate way; giving generously as well as receiving graciously from others.

Adaptability – Being flexible and adaptable to accomplish what needs to be done; understanding your own impact on others in a situation and adjusting the way in which you engage with and support them to succeed; being self-confident and assured as well as open and receptive.

Authenticity – Real, open and genuine in presenting who you are and what is important to you to the world; acknowledging that you bring unique perspective and insights to people and situations and being willing to share these, with humility, for the benefit of others.

Synthesis – Able to bring all the component pieces together to both create and understand the whole; noticing and gathering information about what is happening at a number of different 'layers' in a situation, including with the people involved; integrating all of this information to create meaning and understanding for others.

Continuity – Able to build and maintain a sustainable position for the future, both for yourself and others; balancing the desire for stability in systems with measured and calculated risk taking; looking for opportunities to strengthen consistency in processes with continuous improvement.

Seeing potential – Able to envision the potential and possibilities in yourself, others and situations around you; inspiring others with 'what could be' and bringing optimism to the achievement of what is possible.

Having identified those leadership distinctions that feel most 'like you', take some time to look back through the distinctions and consider those that are *less* familiar to you – those that you feel you are less likely to incorporate into the ways you lead and engage others, and in particular those that you would like to see or feel more of in yourself.

The aim in increasing our emotional health levels is to have access to the qualities and characteristics of all nine of these distinctions, effectively 'on demand'. We call this expanding our 'behavioural freedom' – which is what we will explain next.

Emotional health levels

The concept of 'emotional health levels' takes the previous notions of personal responsibility (the line of choice), whole body thinking (the centres of intelligence) and the leadership distinctions a few steps further. Understanding this will establish an important step towards increasing your level of emotional health, that is, staying above the line, integrating all three centres of intelligence and embracing all the leadership distinctions.

Emotional health levels are illustrated in Figure 3.

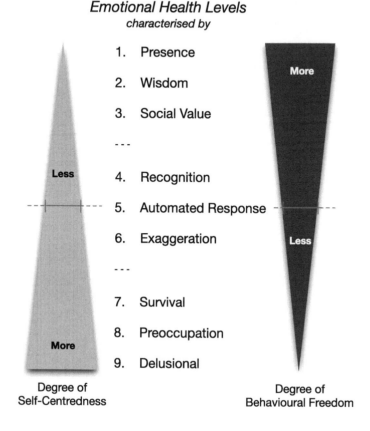

Emotional Health Levels
characterised by

1. Presence
2. Wisdom
3. Social Value
- - -
4. Recognition
5. Automated Response
6. Exaggeration
- - -
7. Survival
8. Preoccupation
9. Delusional

Less / More (Degree of Self-Centredness)

More / Less (Degree of Behavioural Freedom)

Degree of
Self-Centredness

Degree of
Behavioural Freedom

Figure 3: Emotional health levels (adapted from the work of Don Riso and Russ Hudson, 1999).

In this model, the triangle on the left shows the 'degree of self-centredness' for people at different emotional health levels (the maximum being at level 9). This is the degree to which we are specifically focused on ourselves to ensure that we will survive in our environment. As such it also represents the degree to which we engage our defence mechanisms in an attempt to make sure we will feel safe.

The triangle on the right indicates the 'degree of behavioural freedom' for people at different emotional health levels (the maximum being at level 1). This is the degree to which we are able to choose our behaviours in response to any given situation.

The way we like to explain this model is to start at the middle level and then describe the differences we see as we move up and down from there. Later we'll provide more detail on some of the levels.

Let's take a hypothetical leader who is centred at level 5 on this diagram (we would say this person has an emotional health level of 5). This is the level which would be represented by much of the Western world's leadership.

At this level this person wants to have a 'good' life with friends, a steady job with leadership aspirations, a comfortable place to live and the ability to spend time on leisure activities and relaxing as well as work – all of this is likely to be familiar to you.

Our 'level 5' leader[2] will react thoughtfully to some of the situations that they find themselves in, thinking as much about others as they do about themselves. However, there will be other

---

[2] Our description of a leader at emotional health level 5 is not to be confused with the 'Level 5 leader' described by Jim Collins in his inspiring book, *Good to Great*. Collins's concept of 'levels' is quite separate from ours. However, it is worth noting that Collins's 'Level 5 leader' would most likely be someone with a high level of emotional health – probably at least level 3.

times when this leader will respond to situations in ways that are quite reactive and without thought. Their response or reaction in that moment will be what we described earlier as 'automatic' or 'below the line', with blaming, denying, defending and justifying appearing in the mix. It is likely to be those who are very close to this leader who will push their 'hot buttons' and trigger such behaviours. (You are probably familiar with this also.)

When a leader reacts like this, they have not consciously thought about what they did or said; they have just reacted. In terms of our model, we would say that at the point of reaction their 'degree of behavioural freedom' was limited. In other words, they did not think about the best response – they literally just reacted.

It is generally possible to recognise and observe this type of 'below-the-line' reactive response in ourselves and others, if only in retrospect. It is interesting to note that a level 5 leader will often regret 'below-the-line' behaviour afterwards. They will realise that they did not think before they acted and, as a result, did not choose the best response to their situation. However, this realisation is often too late.

These reactive behaviours are often the easiest to see and recognise. However, there are multiple layers of automated responses. Let's look at two specific examples: one relating to delegation of tasks and another relating to emotional responses.

If we asked a level 5 leader about the last time they went to delegate a task but didn't, we would likely hear a number of different reasons as to why this had not occurred, reflecting another layer of automated responses. These could include: 'It was quicker and easier to do it myself'; 'No-one else could do it to the standard I want or the way I wanted it done'; or 'My team was already too busy so I did it myself'.

It is almost certain to have been one or more of these 'messages' that had determined the leader's reaction at the time - coming from a high degree of self-centredness and little or no behavioural freedom. This contrasts with other times when the same leader has stopped and reflected before making a choice about what would be best for everyone concerned, drawing on a considered (rather than automated) response that may well have led them to delegate the task to someone else.

For our second example, relating to emotional responses, imagine our level 5 leader has been at a three-day conference. On the last day, at afternoon tea, they meet up with a person who has a passion and interest in the same topic that they do. With only a short time to spend together, the other person agrees to call our leader the following week to arrange a catch-up over coffee. The week comes and goes but the person does not call.

So what does our leader feel? At level 5, there is a full a range of automated emotional responses that can 'show up' in the leader. For example, they can feel that the person didn't really want to meet – they were just being polite on the day, that the person didn't really like them, that the person was not really interested in the topic or that they did not see any value in continuing the contact.

It is one or more of these, or similar, responses that would then automatically guide the leader's reactions.

It would be wrong to see any of these examples as absolute. In practice, different people at the same emotional health level will have different responses – both automated and chosen – depending on their individual makeup or personality. However, the examples should start to give you a sense of the large number of possible automated responses that can be observed in a level 5 leader, many of which both the leader and the casual observer will be unaware of.

As our diagram (Figure 3) illustrates, the top and bottom of the range of emotional health levels represent extremes of behavioural freedom and self-centredness.

A person with an extremely low level of emotional health (level 9) will display automated, 'below-the-line' responses to virtually every situation they encounter. They are so focused on themselves and what they need that they have little or no behavioural freedom to choose their responses to situations. People at this level are often fixated, delusional and self-destructive, and are generally under medical and/ or psychiatric care.

The person with the highest level of emotional health (level 1) is completely open, well balanced and liberated from any degree of self-centredness. With complete behavioural freedom and total integration of all three centres of intelligence, they have complete clarity of thought, are able to make mindful decisions about every situation they encounter and take personal responsibility (remain above the line) for their responses. People at this level define the term 'presence'. We will talk more about this later; suffice to say that they exemplify the qualities and characteristics of all the leadership distinctions and lead by the highest of examples in all aspects of their lives.

It is not our aim in this book to dissect the full range of emotional health levels in great detail, but rather to focus on those levels most commonly found in leadership. Descriptions of these levels (from the somewhat unhealthy level 6 to the quite healthy level 3) will hopefully help you understand how emotional health can change a leader's behaviour and interactions.

At *level 6* (exaggeration) a person can be quite demonstrative in their self-centred, defensive behaviours, with their actions being exaggerated as they over-compensate in response to their internal conflicts and anxieties. The majority of their responses occur automatically, without conscious thought; their thinking takes place largely from the distorted perspective of their preferred centre of intelligence, with only tenuous connection to the other two centres.

From a leadership perspective, at level 6 we see behaviours such as:

- being openly oppositional and uncooperative, refusing to conform to others' expectations

- avoiding getting involved in order to stay out of trouble and conflict

- striving for standards that are nothing short of 'perfect' and rejecting anything that does not meet these

- interfering in situations they could otherwise stay out of, as they believe that others cannot do without their help and constant support

- constantly talking and bragging about themselves to let others know how good they are

- reacting, overanalysing, and imagining others' responses (or lack of them) are all about them

- indirectly undermining others by using their knowledge as a way of unsettling them

- questioning the motives of others and tending to think the worst of people and situations

- being frantically busy and unable to slow down.

Note that in these and the other examples of behaviour below, we would not expect to see the full range of these in any one individual. Some leaders will tend toward a small number of these behaviours, depending on their preference towards particular leadership distinctions, as we discussed earlier.

Building on what we indicated earlier, at *level 5* (automated response) a person is still dominated by a range of automated responses to what is occurring around them. These responses are generally defensive and are concerned with controlling their environment (including the people in it) to try and get their perceived needs met. There are times – more than for level 6 – when they make conscious decisions about their behaviours; however, the automated responses tend to take over when there is any pressure or stress involved.

In leaders at emotional health level 5, we see behaviours such as:

- being blunt and to the point: just saying how it is going to be without factoring in others' feelings

- being too obliging and giving in to others, even if it's not what they really want

- being highly structured and organising and managing their environment to ensure that everything is in the right place

- overextending themselves, helping too many people and feeling burdened as a result

- adjusting their behaviour to suit the particular context so others will think well of them

- having moods that are unpredictable and insisting others respect the delicacy of their feelings

- continuously thinking about and pondering other possibilities and ideas

- overthinking and getting anxious about situations and problems

- not liking to be limited, so being flippant and dismissive of rules and boundaries.

Level 4 (recognition) represents an important shift in emotional health. At this level a person starts to recognise that they have choices with all of their behaviours and begins to observe these on a more regular basis. As this takes place, their level of self-awareness and recognition of their impact on others increases.

To assist in understanding this level, think of a job interview you have been in where you are not only answering the questions being asked by the interviewer, but you are also watching their responses to your answers and adjusting how you will behave or what you might say next as a result. This is the 'inner observer' in action.

The 'inner observer' is the aspect of ourselves that observes what we are thinking, feeling and doing in each moment as those thoughts, feelings and actions are occurring.[3]

Accessing the inner observer gives us the opportunity to make a conscious choice 'in the moment' of what we think is the best thing to do. When we do this, we find ourselves more constructive, calm, relaxed, connected and secure. We are also much more conscious of our current state of being.

At level 4, people tell us that they also experience moments of being 'in presence' or 'in the zone' or 'in the flow'.

It is perhaps easiest to explain this in a sporting context, where the latter two terms are often used. When sportspeople are interviewed

---

[3] For more on this see the article 'Inner Observer Practice' by Ooten, Esposito and O'Hara, Conscious Living Center (2013), at www.goconscious.com/home/articles/inner_observer_practice.html

after achieving great feats, they often describe the psychological state they were in that enabled them to do such amazing things. They will talk in paradoxes. 'I felt relaxed yet every muscle in my body was alert and ready to go.' 'My mind was quiet and still, yet easily able to make immediate decisions as needed.' 'While everything around me was moving quickly I felt as though I had all the time in the world to do what I had to do.' 'There was a timelessness associated with how I felt in this state; everything flowed and I could do no wrong.'

This is very much in contrast to how the same sportspeople might describe their more normal state of play, when they are not 'in the zone'. At these times they might say: 'My body is tense and alert and my muscles ready to go; my mind is full of stuff and busy; everything is moving quickly around me and I feel I do not have time to make the decisions I need to make; everything feels hurried; I often struggle to do the best I can in the circumstances.'

In our own everyday lives we can also experience these moments of being 'in presence'. They can happen in all sorts of places, from walking in the park, sitting in the sun in the garden, walking along a beach, playing with children or pets, listening to music, sitting in a café with friends and many more. (Recall Karenza's descriptions of boxing, and Chris's of bushwalking. Graeme describes meditation as giving him a similar experience.)

During these moments we might experience a very quiet and still mind, where we notice and appreciate everything around us. There is a wonderful sense of inner peace and harmony and being at one with everything – a timelessness about where we are at that moment. We will often reflect on how wonderful it all is and how great it is to be alive.

Then, all of a sudden, we wake out of it. It feels as though it was all a daydream. We are not really sure how long we were in that 'dream', yet we clearly recognise that we were. Parodoxically, this dream-like feeling comes from the fact that while we were in presence we were not consciously aware that we were. We would never think about being in presence while we actually are. Rather we recognise we were in this state when we come out of it and are able to reflect on the beauty and wonder of it all. It's interesting to note that when we are 'in presence' our internal defence mechanisms are not present – we have simply let go of them.

Like sportspeople, business leaders also perform extraordinarily well when they are 'in presence'. However, at level 4 these moments are fleeting. It is only with the application of specific practices and techniques that focus on moving up the emotional health levels (which we will explore in the next section) that such moments can be experienced more often and for longer.

At level 4, people still find it easy to fall into their defence mechanisms and coping strategies. However, the behaviours associated with these are generally more reflective of personal preferences with respect to engaging with the world and tend to have less of a negative impact on others.

From a leadership perspective, behaviours at level 4 can include:

- making choices quickly and confidently and rarely second

guessing themselves

- being calm, not easily affected by events and not hurried or pushed by themselves or others

- having a high set of ideals that they strive to meet at all times

- complimenting and admiring others so they will be recognised themselves

- being so highly focused and goal driven that they put aside feelings to get the job done

- wanting others to recognise and appreciate the qualities that are unique to them

- focusing on a small number of areas to gain mastery and feel competent

- looking to others to validate that they are on the right path

- ensuring that whatever they say is always framed in a positive light.

At *level 3* (social value) a person has significant balance in their life. A sizeable shift occurs in the way in which they see and engage with the world and in their ability to relate to others. With an increased range of behavioural freedom comes the ability to shift their concerns away from themselves and towards others and broader social interests. As their self-centredness decreases there is a natural tendency to embrace the greater good for their communities.

At this level people relate to others through their qualities and strengths in a constructive, mutually beneficial and sustainable way. They see the potential in others and look for opportunities to nurture and support their development, as well as the development of the organisations and communities in which they operate. They spend their time above the line, and operate more often with integrated centres of intelligence.

People at level 3 better understand how they can use their inner observer to further raise their own consciousness. In other words, they start to increase the number of opportunities for 'presence' in their daily living.

In leaders we see behaviours at level 3 such as:

- seeing potential in others and fostering their development and progression

- bringing people together and acting as facilitator in conflicts; finding common ground and solutions

- being directed by truth and justice in what is right for everyone

- being unselfish in sustaining and dignifying the lives of others

- effortlessly communicating what they value in ways that inspire others and promote understanding

- openly sharing what is personal and important to them in order to create greater understanding for everyone

- synthesising data and ideas to create and discover something new and better

- staying on course despite difficulties, obstacles, or discouragement

- having the capacity for high quality work and exemplary delivery of multiple tasks and projects.

# # #

Our three leaders generally see themselves as having an emotional health level centred around level 4, at times using the behaviours of level 3 and on some occasions recognising their automated responses at level 5, particularly in moments of pressure and stress or when their 'hot buttons' are pushed.

Graeme talks quite often about the 'inner observer'. 'I think that the capacity to have the internal observer to reflect back to me why I am feeling the way I am has greatly contributed to me being able to sustain certain positive relationships and do things like ensuring great consistency, which builds integrity, trust and respect for the people you are dealing with.'

Chris's 'inner observer' is also strong, as he constantly monitors his reactions and how he has modified them over time. 'Four or five years ago, early on as I was doing this role, I got described as someone who was "confident bordering on arrogant in a work context".' Now, as he described earlier, his persona at work is much more aligned with his persona at home, and arrogance is not a word anyone would use to describe him.

Karenza describes 'glimpsing' level 3 from time to time – which is helping her gain the confidence to overcome her eating disorder.

Except perhaps at the extremes, no-one lives solely at a single emotional health level. We all have good days and bad days and, as such, most of us will operate at a given level much of the time, while occasionally shifting up or down a level, depending on the circumstances and environment we are in.

Those who move up the emotional health levels over time are better able to see other perspectives of the world they live in; they start to understand the assumptions that their own world-view is built on. As they do this, they better appreciate that the coping strategies and defence mechanisms they have been using are holding back their personal growth. More and more they have the inner observer activated: they appraise their own behaviours and responses, identifying areas of behaviour that could be improved and consciously planning to make these improvements.

Put in terms of the line of choice concept, moving up the emotional health levels means spending more time above the line, and less time below it. It means operating more often with integrated centres of intelligence and spending less time operating out of one's preferred centre of intelligence.

Impact of emotional health levels on results

While the concept of emotional health levels can be applied to any individual, it gains even greater potency when it is applied to leaders.

Almost by definition (referring back to Figure 3), a good leader needs to display a minimum degree of self-centredness (after all, it's about others, the organisation and/or the community, not themselves) and maximum degree of behavioural freedom (in order to make considered decisions rather than automatic or knee-jerk ones).

Leaders are expected to be both compassionate and caring as well as decisive and strong. Achieving this paradox requires a high level of emotional health. We find that leaders from level 4 and above – emotionally healthy leaders such as those we have introduced to you in this book – drive positive emotions in their workplace; they create resonance by inspiring others through the creation of a genuinely shared vision, then coaching them to be all that they can be as they work towards achieving that vision.

It is interesting to note that this ability to create resonance connects with the work outlined by Daniel Goleman in his book *Primal Leadership*.[4] In summary, he shows that higher levels of emotional intelligence in leaders enable the building of more resonant organisations and a corresponding increase in organisation performance.

---

[4] See Daniel Goleman, *Primal Leadership: Learning to Lead with Emotional Intelligence*, Harvard University Press, 2004.

This is not really surprising to us, as the work we have undertaken over the past 10 years has indicated a direct correlation between high levels of emotional intelligence and high levels of emotional health. That is, as we move up the emotional health levels we also increase our levels of emotional intelligence, along with other things, including the breadth of our perspectives on the world and the extent to which we integrate all three centres of intelligence.

We have also found that high emotional health levels have positive and significant effects on team and organisational performance across a range of measures. We will share more about our findings in these areas in future publications.

For now, the question is what can be done to increase one's emotional health level. How can you, as a leader, become more emotionally healthy – and a great leader as a result?

Part 3: Becoming an Emotionally Healthy Leader

At the start of this book we asked you to bring into your mind some of the leaders you have most admired. We asked you not to try and analyse them but instead just have them sit with you as reminders of what leadership can be when it is done 'right'. Our strong suspicion is that if you pause now and take a fresh look back at those leaders, you will see many of the characteristics that we have been describing so far: taking personal responsibility with above-the-line responses; whole body thinking through a balance of the head, heart and 'gut' centres; and incorporation of a wide range of the nine leadership distinctions into the way they led and engaged others.

In the introduction we also shared our belief that emotionally healthy leadership can provide a path that will change the way you engage and work with others and strengthen your value as a leader. To be more specific, there are real and tangible benefits for you as a leader in moving up the emotional health levels:

- Your 'inner observer' enables you to be very aware of your own responses and reactions and their impact on others.

- You become much clearer about what is important to you in the way you lead and engage others, as well as becoming clearer about what is important to them.

- Your perspective on life, leadership and the world expands as you become more open to the possibilities around you.

- You recognise there are multiple perspectives on any given situation, and you are able to determine the best course of action free of personal attachment to any particular one.

- You are able to make conscious choices to increase the number and duration of 'moments of presence' in your life, and as a result realise the full extent of your amazing potential.

- You can simplify complex ideas, scenarios and situations and so enable others to navigate through this environment with ease.

So, what do you need to be doing as a leader to increase your emotional health?

We've already noted that emotionally healthy leadership won't come simply by learning a new set of skills. Increasing your emotional health level can't be done by reading a book, or by cognitively understanding the behaviours and qualities that exist at higher health levels.

If we focus for a moment on the centres of intelligence perhaps we can explain what we mean.

We introduced the centres in terms of three different ways of thinking and the way each of us has a tendency to draw on one of these – instinct, intuition or insight – more often than the others. We described how increased emotional health is associated with increasing our ability to balance or integrate these three centres and achieve 'whole body thinking'.

However, the centres of intelligence go much deeper than just ways of thinking. They are also centres of *energy*. Truly achieving a balance between the centres means opening up, *exercising* and *experiencing* them. This experience, clearly, can't be achieved cognitively. Put simply, when it comes to balancing the centres *you have to do it to know it*. From this perspective a development path to achieving this balance – and through that increased emotional health – must include a more holistic approach that addresses opening up and connecting to the 'gut', heart and head centres. In particular it must provide improvement and strengthening of each individual's less-connected centres.

A similar argument can be made about development paths towards increasing above-the-line thinking and incorporation of the leadership distinctions: they need to be experiential rather than cognitive. The development path of every individual will be as unique as they are, which reinforces the need for development by personal experience rather than simply appreciating theory and accumulating knowledge.

A complete discussion of development paths towards increased emotional health could be the subject of a book in its own right, and is beyond the scope of what we want to cover here.

What we do want to do is share a range of simple practices and techniques that you can use to build your self-awareness, understanding and connection to all three centres of intelligence. The application of these practices and techniques in a variety of situations over time will give you the foundation you need to increase your emotional health level.

Operating 'above the line'

Back in our original discussion about choosing our responses and the 'line of choice', we pointed out that a good indicator of increased emotional health is the ability to choose to operate 'above the line' more often. We also pointed out that doing this takes practice, particularly as the time between our impulse and our action is only that 'magic quarter second'. Nevertheless, while that makes changing our behaviour seem difficult, with concerted practice this is something that can be achieved quite readily.

Improving your ability to operate above the line requires a good amount of self-reflection.

The first stage is to use hindsight to *calibrate* your understanding of above- and below-the-line reactions as they pertain to you as an individual. You can do this by drawing on your own experiences in the past, or alternatively monitoring your responses to the various situations you find yourself in over the coming week or so and noting down (yes, record or write down) what you experienced, how you reacted and how your reactions affected those around you.

The aim at this stage is not to change your behaviour but simply to better understand the emotional triggers or 'hot buttons' that send you below the line, with their consequent effects on your emotional health.

Start by remembering a situation in which you've been working with a person or a group and everything just seemed to 'click'. Think about what was going on in that situation, about how people were behaving. Was there an overriding sense of respect for each other? Was everyone actively listening to each other? Did each person take responsibility for their own input, and for their own role? Did people tend to think before they responded? Were you doing all these things yourself?

These are the typical behaviours we see when people are operating above the line. If you can recall a good example of such a situation you'll know exactly what we mean.

Try now to recall a situation in which you've worked with another person or group but things were not working nearly so well. A situation in which the default positions of everyone involved – perhaps including yourself – were defensiveness, blame, denial and/ or justification. Think about how people were responding to each other. Did it seem automatic? Were people quick to judge, snapping at each other, acting without thought?

We hardly need to explain what's going on here: that these are typical below-the-line behaviours.

Once you have come up with good examples of these two relative extremes of behaviours above and below the 'line of choice', you will be able to *reflect* on those situations and start to analyse your responses. Quite quickly you will be able to reflect on a broader, less extreme range of situations.

As you reflect on specific situations in which you have responded below the line, ask yourself, 'What is it about this situation that predisposes me to my response?' and note down your answer. With experience this will lead you to an understanding of the patterns or repertoire of your below-the-line responses. This in turn will enable you to identify new ways of responding.

It's important to understand that this isn't about removing the old behaviours – our neural pathways for these are very strong, given their persistent use. However, we do have the ability to create new neural pathways leading to the qualities and characteristics we have previously described at higher emotional health levels (particularly level 3).

The final (and ongoing) stage in training yourself to operate above the line is basically an extension of all we have been discussing so far. Once you are adept at recognising and analysing above and below the line behaviours in yourself with the advantage of hindsight, you should be able to start doing the same thing with more immediacy. We call this 'catching the reaction': becoming aware of your emotions *as* things are unfolding around you, rather than after the event.

Use your notes to identify alternative above-the-line ways of responding to the situations you have been analysing. It can be a good idea to share these with others who you trust and respect and who are close enough to you to observe your behaviour. Asking for their feedback on how you are going becomes a critical part of making progress. It is also one of the hallmarks of an emotionally healthy leader – being open and vulnerable to ideas and suggestions from others on how you can improve and develop.

Several leaders we work with have created a personal flip chart describing the triggers and situations that tend to send them below the line, causing their default reactions and defensive behaviours to surface. They then indicate specific above-the-line behaviours and qualities that they plan to use in future in similar situations, including how those behaviours and qualities will look in action. They keep this flip chart with them in their workplace and use it as an opportunity to receive feedback from others as part of their development.

Over time, with continuous conscious effort and practice, the need for physical reminders will diminish – above-the-line responses will increasingly become second nature as new neural pathways establish themselves. However, it is important to understand that this occurs progressively over time – not overnight.

Having a clear 'intent'

A very common question of a leader in relation to their own development would be 'What do you want to achieve (that is "to do")?', to which the response is usually something about taking action or implementing a new activity.

We ask a very different question when working with leaders on the path to increasing their emotional health. The question is, 'How do you want to *be* or *be seen*?'. The answers to this question are completely different to those of the earlier question. They typically invoke words like 'confident', 'inspiring' or 'engaging' – words that can completely change the way a leader presents and works with others.

What is being demonstrated in the difference between these two questions, and their subsequent answers, is the difference between 'intention' and 'intent'.

Good intentions are the way most of us navigate our days, months and even careers. An intention in the office might be to finish the to-do list, or complete a particular project. The intention for a facilitator heading into a workshop might be to receive high evaluation scores, or to finish on time.

An 'intention' is something you hope to *do*. 'Hope' is an important word here, because intentions tend to be about hope. Intentions are about 'try' and 'should' and 'might'. Intentions are what many politicians, business people and others often have when they make statements about being 'committed' to some outcome.

The concept of 'intent' is much stronger and deeper than intention. Intent is about a state of mind – one that comes with earnest purpose. It's about how we want to *be* or *be seen*, rather than simply what we want to do. Intent is about establishing a designated quality or behaviour, which in turn creates appropriate actions consistent with that quality.

As an example, if we are co-facilitating a workshop, prior to the start we will often privately share an intent to be 'seamless'. We don't communicate this intent publicly with the workshop participants, yet often someone will come up to us, unprompted, during the day and comment on how seamlessly we work together – using that exact word. The same thing often happens when we share an intent to be 'collaborative'.

On a broader scale, it is intent that keeps our organisation on track, year after year. When we set up Global Leadership Foundation our intent was threefold: to be self-realised, collaborative and stewards for community (environment, social, local and global). This intent has constantly guided our decision making and presented opportunities that are in tune with how we want our organisation to be.

Introducing the notion of intent to your life is not difficult, and there are some simple and effective ways to begin.

When starting out, the best action to take is to state your intent each morning for the day ahead. Do this by choosing a word or words (ideally from those you have identified in the above-the-line process) that describe the way you would like to *be* today. Prompt yourself by asking a question of intent like: 'How do I want to be in the meeting today?'; 'How do I want to engage with my team?'; or 'How do I want to be as I meet the shareholders?'. Words like 'confident', 'inspiring', 'engaging', 'relaxed', or 'connected' will often appear in response to questions like this.

If your day will be spent in your office – you have a report to write, for instance – your intent might be something like 'focused', or 'calm', or 'clear'.

Of course, all these words are only suggestions and we encourage you to explore the summaries of the nine leadership distinctions (on page 69) and the descriptors at emotional health level 3 (on page 84) for more ideas.

The trick in stating your intent is to keep it short: one or two words are preferable. Also, make sure you choose words that have 'real' meaning relating to the way you want to be and how others will experience you – not what you want to do. There is a difference.

When stating your intent, it must be verbalised. Your intent must 'leave your head'. A good way to do this is to tell someone else: your partner or a trusted work colleague. (Ideally in this case you will share each other's intents.) If you can't share your intent with someone else, send a voicemail to yourself. Or just say it out loud: dogs and cats can be good listeners. Other strategies are to write your intent on a piece of paper – any piece of paper – or to write it in a journal. Journals can be a good way of tracking your intent over time.

That said, don't actively review your intent. This point can be hard to comprehend for many who hold fast to the precept of 'You manage what you measure'. However, the point of stating an intent is *not* to constantly remind yourself of it during the day, nor to mechanistically review its success or otherwise at the end of the day. It is about embodying how you want to be. You'll know if you've been effective. Look for signs in others: the glint in the eye of someone you are working with, or a newfound enthusiasm in one of your team.

Like learning to operate above the line, all of this takes time and practice. It is important that you stick at it. Don't expect instant results and never expect specific results – 'If I act with confidence I will get that deal'. Rather, get into the habit of stating your intent every day and, over time, you will start to notice the impact it is having.

It has to be said that for some people this can be difficult. Many leaders require support or coaching through the initial stages, either to help them identify the right words for their intent, or to help them see success in terms of increased emotional health rather than 'tangible' outcomes.

EnneaMotion

Our colleague and friend Andrea Isaacs has developed a unique approach to increasing emotional health known as 'EnneaMotion'[5] – the use of simple movement exercises to explore the energy of different centres of intelligence and their characteristics.

EnneaMotion enables us to take intent to a new level by embodying 'how we want to be' in our physical being – that is, 'putting ourselves in the experience'.

Let's start with a story to demonstrate what we mean. Imagine you are going to a special dinner. You have purchased a new outfit for this occasion and when you get dressed that evening you look in the mirror and go, 'Wow!' You look and feel like a 'million dollars'.

[5] Learn more about EnneaMotion at www.enneamotion.com.

So what happens to the way you are standing, to the way you walk, to your facial expressions? More than likely you stand tall. You 'strut' rather than walk; you smile. Other people comment on how confident and great you look. This is not just about your new clothes – it is about your whole being. Your feelings – mainly confidence in this instance – are embodied in how you 'present'.

EnneaMotion provides the same opportunity to make choices about the way you want to be, and to create that.

According to Andrea, EnneaMotion 'technically uses a movement vocabulary of space, time and energy that allows us to name and classify the physical movement components that accompany each thought or emotion. For example, if we're angry, we're probably moving in a sharp, fast, direct, forceful and angular way. If we're depressed or sad, we might move in a manner that is slow, limp, unfocused and weak, or be almost still. Confidence could be translated as direct and forceful; nurturing could be translated as indirect and gentle. Each thought and feeling has its exact counterpart in the physical realm'.

EnneaMotion provides the opportunity to recognise below-the-line moments, create new pathways (intent) in response to them and then 'experience' the benefits by embedding these new pathways through movement. Andrea asks us to imagine a situation in which 'you feel angry at your friend and would like to stop feeling that way. You may tell yourself, "Stop it," but if you find yourself yelling at your dog for no reason, minutes later, you know that you have simply shifted your anger onto a different object. Imagine that, instead, you briefly stop and notice how you are moving (sharp, fast, direct, forceful and angular) then try to move in the opposite manner for a minute or two (vague, slow, indirect, gentle and round). You would immediately notice how this 'opposite' set of movements makes it difficult to remember why you were angry, let alone still feel it.'

This is a powerful way of associating physical reactions with emotional responses, and thereby playing a role in increasing your emotional health.

While you may need more guidance than we have provided here in order to make full use of EnneaMotion, a first step is simply to notice how you are feeling, connect this with the way your body is responding (whether above or below the line) and record it – much as we suggested with 'catching the reaction' earlier. Identify the emotions and physical reactions (e.g. body language) and then begin to explore shifting your body language to the opposite for below-the-line responses. Or try to recreate the same physical experience for above-the-line responses.

Thinking with your 'whole body'

We have already discussed the centres of intelligence and 'whole body thinking' at some length, so will not restate that background here. Suffice to say that integrating and bringing full attention to all three centres of intelligence – the 'gut', heart and head – enables us to increase our range of behavioural freedom and access the leadership distinctions we have previously described. It also increases the opportunity to be more 'in the moment' than not, and furthers our practice in being 'in the zone' or 'in the flow' – that is, in 'presence'. All of this lies at the core of moving up the emotional health levels.

In terms of practices and techniques you can use to increasingly integrate the three centres for yourself, there are many options available.

Eastern cultures have practised this for thousands of years through meditation, yoga, martial arts, tai chi, qigong and so on.

You can also remove your shoes and walk quietly along a beach; sit under a tree in a park or forest and notice the sounds around you; take in an amazing view at the top of a hill, lookout or mountain; watch dolphins leaping and cavorting alongside a boat; play in the sun with your children or pet; lie on the grass and simply close your eyes and notice the smells. All of these and similar activities can increase the integration of your centres.

However, even when all of these seem remote possibilities, with the world of work right in front of you, there are still practices you can adopt to engage all three centres.

If you notice that you are over-analysing something, have too many ideas or suggestions to consider, or are relying on others to provide their thoughts and ideas instead of coming up with your own – all of these are indicators that you may be out of touch with your 'body' centre. You can ground your 'gut' feelings – your instinct – simply by sitting upright on a chair with both feet on the floor, your hands flat on your knees and your eyes closed (or looking at the floor and 'blurring' your focus).

A good way to stay connected with the instinct centre and encourage a quiet mind is via regular exercise. We've described the way the leaders in this book do that with running, walking, swimming and even boxing, but many other leaders we know also use exercise regimes to keep themselves grounded. Of course there are hundreds of options – you just need to find something you can do regularly and enjoyably.

Feeling judgemental about another person in a meeting, or having difficulty understanding where another person is coming from in terms of how they are expressing themselves, are both signs that you may be out of touch with your heart centre. A very straightforward 'connecting' activity in this instance is to lean forward on your chair, with an elbow on the table and hand on your chest as you look around at the others in the room. This will help you reconnect to your feelings and intuition.

Again, many leaders we know use specific practices to connect with their heart centre. Karenza identified the important use of music to set the scene prior to meeting people, which enables her to be calm and connected in the space. A more sophisticated practice is the use of singing bowls and tuning forks tuned to a frequency that opens the heart connection.[6]

---

[6] Joshua Leeds, *The Power of Sound: How to Be Healthy and Productive Using Music and Sound*, Healing Arts Press, 2010.

Alternatively, simply creating opportunities for social engagement can also open up and maintain your connection to the heart centre. This is even easier when it involves an activity you are passionate about. For instance, if you love the outdoors then consider joining a walking club; if you enjoy music and singing then find a choir to get involved with.

Finally, if you find yourself struggling for awareness about or understanding of a situation, or you need to make sense of a large amount of information or data you are receiving, you may have lost connection with your head centre. An easy technique for remedying this at your desk involves putting your elbow on the table and cupping your chin in your hand. It's amazing how this simple 'clearing' activity can clarify your thoughts and provide fresh insight.

Interestingly, many of the leaders we know find that connecting to the head centre often requires them to get rid of the mental chatter first. They therefore begin the process of connection by using techniques and practices from the other two centres, say taking a walk and/or playing a piece of music, which helps them to become calm, relaxed and clear.

Time and practice will be your friends again when it comes to integrating your centres of intelligence. The nice thing about the techniques described here, however, is that they are mostly proactive and don't require you to 'catch the reaction'. Simply building practices that promote connection to all three centres into your daily or weekly routine will, over time, promote greater balance.

Expanding 'behavioural freedom'

Consistently applying the practices and techniques we have described so far will provide opportunities to increase your access to all nine of the leadership distinctions, thereby expanding your 'behavioural freedom'.

As your thinking becomes clearer and as you start to find yourself having more time and space to analyse the way you are engaging with others, you will be able to identify and focus on those distinctions you want to strengthen. You will be able to call upon those distinctions more often and for longer.

The more you are able to lead and engage others by accessing the full range of leadership distinctions, the more emotionally healthy you will become as a leader.

Coaching and mentoring

All three of our leaders recognise the importance that external support has played in their ability to increase their emotional health levels. This support can come from the environment in which they work – the overall culture of the organisation. Sometimes it comes from another leader or manager who saw something in them and was willing to give them a chance. Sometimes it comes from the staff they have managed: those willing to accept their leader's vulnerabilities when they were brave enough to share them.

These leaders, along with many others with whom we have

worked, also recognise the important role that a coach or mentor can play in supporting their ongoing development in emotional health. Sitting with a trusted person to explore the current assumptions and related behaviours a leader holds, and the automated patterns that appear in different situations, provides safe feedback on how effective (or otherwise) these are. It can also reveal alternative ways of overcoming any negative or below-the-line behaviours. It can help identify disconnection with particular centres of intelligence and strategies for reconnecting.

As you embark on increasing your level of emotional health, you may uncover a range of automated behaviours you haven't recognised in yourself previously. This is quite common. As a result, you may feel initially (but usually incorrectly) that you are moving back down the emotional health levels rather than up. This experience is the result of your newfound ability to distinguish many more of the patterns and triggers associated with these responses. Put simply, the more you know, the more you are realising how much you don't know. Having a coach or mentor to check in with and provide you with feedback on the accuracy of your self-assessment can provide a very important benefit in this phase.

When choosing a coach or mentor to support you in this process, it is important to consider their own emotional health level as well. We would suggest that you choose someone you consider to be emotionally healthy – someone at level 4 as a minimum. The behavioural descriptors for levels 3 and 4 (see from page 82) also provide a good reference for selecting a person who can be of value to you. It may be helpful to consider finding someone who is strong and emotionally healthy in the distinction or distinctions you would like to develop.

Final Words

We introduced this book by painting a portrait based on three emotionally healthy leaders. Each is unique (as are the leaders we initially asked you to reflect on), however what is common and binds them together is the way in which they lead and engage others.

In the world of leadership there is increasing recognition of a distinction between 'horizontal' capability – the widely taught base skills, abilities and behaviours of leadership – and 'vertical' development, which is essential to sustainable, empowering leadership. It is vertical development, not horizontal capability, that differentiates great leadership from good leadership.

Vertical development refers to the internal growth of a leader: improvement in the way the leader relates to, leads and engages others. These are precisely what emerges from moving up the emotional health levels.

As we have shown, emotional health is defined by a range of characteristics and behaviours that can't be learnt simply by 'thinking' or 'knowing' about them. Moving up the emotional health levels requires leaders to be in the moment of their own experiences. They need to be increasingly self-aware and understanding of their own responses and reactions. They need to understand the impact they have on others as they choose their next course of action.

What we have offered in this book is some of the knowledge you will need, and a range of practices and techniques you can use, to improve your level of emotional health. What is here is only a fraction of what is available to you; however, we know that it is enough to work with and put to good use in both your role as a leader and other aspects of your life.

All of this, as we have said a number of times, takes time and dedication. It requires resilience – everyone comes up against barriers to growth at different times in their lives. It also requires support – not everyone has the capacity to move past these barriers with just determination and persistence.

At the same time, any progress is worthwhile progress, so from the very first time you catch yourself dropping below the line, you should pat yourself on the back. You are on your way!

Of course, increasing your emotional health is not just about you. Quite the contrary: increasing your emotional health has a direct and positive impact on the people you work with and lead, on the business or organisation you work in, and on the people you live with and love.

Emotional health is central to the way in which we engage, collaborate and work with others. As you move up the health levels your focus on the true value of collaboration (that is, achieving success with and through others for the greater good) will be realised. The potential to take these opportunities further into communities, countries and for our planet as a whole (that is, through stewardship) will also be fulfilled. We will explore both these ideas in more depth in future books in this series.

If *this* book has helped set you on a journey towards further developing you as a leader, then we have succeeded in our goal.

About the authors

As the co-founders of Global Leadership Foundation, Gayle Hardie and Malcolm Lazenby are passionate about making a positive difference to people's lives, their businesses and communities – both local and global.

Along with their enthusiasm, Gayle and Malcolm bring over 30 years of experience and recognised expertise in: leadership development and transformation; emotional health and leadership resilience; strategic planning and implementation; organisation and cultural transformation; and board and executive mentoring and coaching.

Gayle and Malcolm's work on the emotional health levels of leaders and their 'translation' of the Enneagram (the study of nine basic personality types and their interrelationship) into practical and tangible business applications are recognised across the globe as both innovative and groundbreaking.

Gayle has a Bachelor of Science in Human Relations and Organisational Behaviour and a Master of Arts (minor in Psychology). She has held significant roles in both the public and private sectors focusing on organisation development and change and strengthening community leadership.

Among other achievements, Gayle is a Fellow and former board member of Leadership Victoria and is a recipient of the Business and Professional Women's Community Leadership Award.

Malcolm has a Bachelor of Education and a Graduate Diploma in Human Resource Management. His skills were strengthened through senior leadership and management roles in the service sector and significant consulting experience in leadership development, organisational transformation and emotional intelligence.

Malcolm's work in the application and measurement of Emotional Intelligence within an Australian business environment is recognised as leading edge and he continues to be approached by researchers (particularly from the USA) to use his evaluation methodology.

Profit for a purpose

Global Leadership Foundation leads by example in its stewardship role, supporting a number of community programmes and not-for-profit organisations as volunteers, facilitators, mentors and philanthropists.

Global Leadership Foundation has also partnered with the Australian Communities Foundation to establish a tax-deductible fund for the development of leaders in communities. The profits of Global Leadership Foundation's corporate work are added to this fund on an annual basis.

GlobaLeadership Foundation™

Global Leadership Foundation was formed in 2003 with the intent of raising emotional health levels across the globe. To achieve this, we develop, strengthen and transform the leadership potential in people, organisations and communities.

Our guiding principles of Self-Realisation, Collaboration and Stewardship underpin the way in which we work and the way we engage with others.

Each of these principles impacts on and influences the other. As a person gains insight in one of these areas, the significance of the connection to the others becomes apparent.

Global Leadership Foundation is recognised for its significant contribution to the development of transformational leadership programs within the private, professional, community and public sectors.

We work with executives, board members and managers in these sectors to help develop and transform them into capable, empathic and effective leaders.

Our work includes:

- **mentoring senior leaders** in the planning, development and sponsorship of leadership programs

- facilitating, planning and implementation support in the areas of **strategic direction, planning and structural review**. This includes mentoring and supporting boards as they review their strategic plans and performance

- supporting **organisation renewal and cultural transformation** using an innovative and collaborative approach to organisation change. This approach has made a difference at all levels of government, as well as in the private, not-for-profit and professional sectors

- **building leadership capacity** within the team environment, specifically working with 'teams at the top' and acknowledging the dilemma of needing to meet organisational expectations at a divisional or partner level, as well as needing to collaborate and work together across the organisation to achieve success

- **building leadership brand** that enables leaders to distinguish the strengths they have, what they want to be known for and how they want to operate in the world of work

- contributing to and engaging leaders in a number of **ecologically and community-based leadership programs and experiences**, which include volunteering, facilitating, coaching and mentoring roles

- **coaching and mentoring** board members and senior executives across Australia and globally

- **developing and facilitating specific programs** to meet identified needs at an organization or community level.

Many of these unique approaches to leadership and culture integrate the Enneagram – an important tool for understanding what drives and motivates individuals, teams, organisations and cultures.

Global Leadership Foundation is recognised for translating the Enneagram into business applications. We are often invited to share our knowledge with clients and at conferences across Australia and around the world.

For more information about Global Leadership Foundation and how we can assist with the growth of emotional healthy leadership in your organisation, visit **www.globalleadershipfoundation.com**

15111527R00072

Printed in Great Britain
by Amazon.co.uk, Ltd.,
Marston Gate.